Empowering Young Girls in Flag Football: A Comprehensive Guide

By Tommie Wamack

TABLE OF CONTENTS

FOREWORD

This book is your passport to the exciting world of flag football, where we aim to empower aspiring young female players with the knowledge, skills, and unwavering confidence needed to excel in the sport. Whether you're a beginner curious about the essence of flag football or a seasoned player looking to master advanced strategies, this guide is your ultimate resource.

Flag football is more than just a game; it's a platform for growth, empowerment, and limitless potential. As we embark on this journey together, we will explore every facet of flag football, from its rich history to the cutting-edge techniques that will help you rise above the competition.

Throughout these pages, you'll discover not only the rules and tactics of the game but also the values of teamwork, sportsmanship, and resilience that extend beyond the field. We'll provide the tools to develop your physical abilities, mental fortitude, and leadership skills.

As we delve into each chapter, you'll understand the sport deeply, learn how to work cohesively with your teammates and harness your inner strength to overcome challenges.

Whether you dream of scoring touchdowns, making crucial flag pulls, or inspiring future generations of female flag football players, this guide is your blueprint for success.

Remember, flag football is about more than just winning; it's about self-discovery, personal growth, and empowering young girls everywhere. With dedication, perseverance, and the knowledge contained within these pages, you can become a skilled and confident flag football player and a symbol of inspiration for others.

So, lace up your cleats, put on that flag belt, and let's step onto the field together. It's time to empower young girls to shine in the thrilling world of flag football.

CHAPTER 1
Understanding Flag Football

In this introductory chapter, we will embark on a journey to understand the essence of flag football. We'll explore its history, compare it to tackle football and celebrate the inclusive nature of this captivating sport.

1.1 The History and Evolution of Flag Football

As we know it today, flag football has a fascinating history deeply rooted in American football's tradition. Significant milestones have marked its evolution from a casual recreational activity to a competitive sport.

Origins: Flag football's roots can be traced to the early 20th century when it emerged as a less physically demanding alternative to tackle football. It was often played in backyards, parks, and military bases, providing a safer way for individuals to enjoy the excitement of football without the full-contact aspect. Its accessibility and lower risk of injury made it an attractive option for people of all ages and backgrounds.

Development: Over the decades, flag football transformed an informal pastime into an organized and structured sport. Leagues and tournaments dedicated to flag football began to emerge, offering players a chance to compete at various levels. The sport's growth is a testament to its adaptability and enduring appeal.

Key Milestones: Throughout its history, flag football has achieved key milestones that have shaped its development. These include the establishment of official rules, the formation of national and international flag football organizations, and the inclusion of flag football in multi-sport events. These milestones have elevated the sport's status and paved the way for greater recognition and participation.

Understanding the history of flag football provides a context that allows players, coaches, and enthusiasts to appreciate the sport's journey and the passion that has driven its evolution.

1.2 Flag Football vs. Tackle Football

Although both are rooted in American football, flag and tackle football offer distinct experiences and cater to different preferences and priorities.

Safety: One of the most significant advantages of flag football is its emphasis on safety. By eliminating physical tackling, flag football drastically reduces the risk of injuries, making it an attractive option for individuals and parents concerned about player safety. This focus on safety aligns with modern concerns about sports-related injuries, particularly in youth sports.

Accessibility: Flag football is highly accessible and inclusive. It is a sport that welcomes individuals of all ages, genders, and skill levels. The absence of full-contact tackling allows people who might not consider tackling football due to physical or safety concerns to enjoy the excitement of football.

Inclusivity: Flag football is a trailblazer promoting inclusivity and gender equality in sports. Removing the barrier of tackling opens the doors to both male and female players, fostering an environment where everyone can compete on an equal footing. This inclusivity challenges traditional gender stereotypes in sports and contributes to a more diverse and equitable sporting landscape.

Skill Development: While flag football eliminates tackling, it strongly focuses on developing essential football skills. Players pass, receive, and flag-pulling, honing fundamental transferable abilities to tackle football and other sports. This skill development aspect prepares players for future endeavors and enhances their overall athletic abilities.

Understanding these distinctions between flag football and tackle football allows individuals to make informed choices based on their preferences and priorities. It also highlights the role of flag football in promoting inclusivity and safety in sports.

1.3 The Inclusivity of Flag Football

Flag football's commitment to inclusivity sets it apart as a sport that values diversity and welcomes individuals from all walks of life. This section celebrates this inclusivity and shares stories that exemplify its impact.

Inclusive Sport: Flag football transcends traditional gender norms and welcomes players of all backgrounds, abilities, and identities. It is a beacon of inclusivity in sports, fostering an environment where diversity and differences are united.

Empowering Girls: Female flag football players have shattered stereotypes and achieved remarkable success. Their stories of resilience, determination, and achievement are potent sources of inspiration for aspiring young girls. These role models demonstrate no limits to what girls can achieve in sports.

Community and Support: Flag football communities often go beyond the game, fostering a sense of belonging and support. Organizations, teams, and districts are instrumental in creating environments where players can thrive as athletes and individuals. They provide a network of encouragement and camaraderie that extends well beyond the field.

Recognizing and celebrating flag football's inclusivity highlights its role as a sport and a platform for social change. It empowers individuals, promotes equality, and fosters a sense of belonging, making it a sport that goes beyond the scoreboards and profoundly impacts the lives of its participants.

By understanding the history, distinguishing features, and inclusivity of flag football, individuals can appreciate the sport's unique charm and potential to empower young girls both on and off the field. The following chapters will delve deeper into the mechanics, strategies, and skills needed to thrive in this thrilling and inclusive game.

CHAPTER 2
Rules and Regulations

In Chapter 2, we will dive deep into the essential rules and regulations governing flag football. A solid understanding of these rules is crucial for players and fans to enjoy a fair and exciting match. Additionally, we will explore the role of officials and emphasize the importance of safety measures within the sport.

2.1 Flag Football Rules

Flag football is a dynamic sport with a unique set of rules that distinguish it from other forms of football. A comprehensive understanding of these rules is essential for players, coaches, and fans.

Let's explore these rules in detail:

❖ **Scoring:** In flag football, points through touchdowns, conversions, and field goals. A touchdown is the most significant scoring play, awarding the offensive team six points when a player successfully carries the ball across the opposing team's goal line. Conversions offer an opportunity to gain additional points, typically one or two, depending on the distance from the goal line—field goals, though less common in flag football, provide three points when executed successfully.

❖ **Game Duration:** A typical flag football game has four quarters or two halves, with each period lasting a specified amount of time. Halftime separates the two halves. Use overtime periods to determine the winner of a tied game at the end of regulation time.

❖ **Timeouts:** Teams have limited timeouts to use during a game. These timeouts serve various strategic purposes, allowing teams to regroup, plan plays or manage the game clock. Coaches and players must use timeouts judiciously, as they can be valuable in critical situations.

❖ **Flag Pulling:** Flag pulling is the primary method of ending a play in flag football. Defensive players attempt to remove a ball carrier's flag to "tackle" them. When a flag is pulled, the play is over, and the ball is spotted at the location of the flag pull. This rule eliminates the physical contact in tackle football, making flag football a safer alternative.

❖ **Player Eligibility:** Flag football has rules governing player eligibility and positioning. These rules ensure teams have an equal opportunity to compete. They dictate which players are eligible to receive passes and their positions on the field.

❖ **Illegal contact:** Flag football has rules against illegal contact, such as blocking, holding, and rough play. These rules prevent aggressive or dangerous actions and promote sportsmanship.

❖ **Passing and Receiving:** Flag football features specific rules governing passes, catches, interceptions, and incomplete passes. Understanding these rules is crucial for offensive and defensive players, as they influence the outcome of plays.

Comprehending these rules is not just a matter of following the game; it's a fundamental aspect of playing flag football with integrity. Knowing the rules allows players to make informed decisions on the field, strategize effectively, and respect the spirit of fair competition.

2.2   Officiating the Game

Referees and officials are the unsung heroes of flag football, ensuring that the games are played according to the rules. Let's delve deeper into their roles and responsibilities:

❖ **Referee Roles:** Various officials fulfill different roles in a flag football game. The head referee oversees the game's overall flow and makes critical decisions. Line judges assist in making calls along the sidelines, while timekeepers manage the game clock and play clock.

❖ **Enforcing Rules:** Officials are responsible for enforcing the rules of flag football. They judge flag pulls, pass interference, and other infractions. Their role is essential in maintaining the integrity of the game and ensuring that all participants adhere to the established regulations.

❖ **Respect for Officials:** Players, coaches, and spectators must respect officials' authority and decisions. While disagreements may arise, respecting officials' decisions is vital for maintaining a positive and sportsmanlike atmosphere. Challenging calls should be done through proper channels and with respect for the game's integrity.

❖ **Challenges and Disputes:** In some cases, coaches may have the option to challenge specific calls or rulings made by officials. These challenges are governed by specific rules and procedures to ensure fairness and accuracy. Resolving disputes on the field is crucial to the game's smooth progression.

Understanding the role of officials and respecting their decisions is not just a matter of etiquette but a fundamental aspect of sportsmanship. Officials work diligently to ensure a fair and enjoyable game, and their efforts should be acknowledged and appreciated.

2.3 Safety Measures

Safety is paramount in flag football, and the sport takes various measures to protect players from injuries. Let's explore these safety measures in more detail:

❖ **Necessary Equipment:** Flag football requires specific equipment to ensure ball carriers wear player safety. Flag belts and flags attached to the belts. Mouthguards are recommended to protect against accidental collisions or falls. Appropriate footwear, such as cleats for turf or grass, helps prevent slips and injuries.

❖ **Helmets and Pads:** Unlike tackle football, where helmets and protective pads are standard equipment, flag football typically does not require players to wear helmets or pads. The absence of these items aligns with the reduced physical contact in the sport.

❖ **Common Penalties:** Flag football has rules to discourage dangerous plays and unsportsmanlike conduct. Penalties are assessed for infractions such as rough play, illegal contact, and dishonest behavior. Understanding these penalties and their consequences promotes fair play and player safety.

❖ **Injury Prevention:** Injury prevention is a priority in flag football. Players are encouraged to engage in proper warm-up exercises to prepare their bodies for physical activity. Staying hydrated is essential to prevent heat-related issues. Coaches often emphasize safe tackling techniques, even though tackling is flag-based rather than physical.

Prioritizing safety protects players from injuries and contributes to a positive and enjoyable flag football experience for all participants. It underscores the sport's commitment to creating an environment where players can compete safely and confidently.

By understanding the rules and regulations of flag football, respecting the role of officials, and prioritizing safety, players can engage in this thrilling sport with confidence, integrity, and a commitment to fair play. In the upcoming chapters, we will delve deeper into the fundamental aspects of flag football and the skills required to excel on the field.

CHAPTER 3
Basics of Flag Football

In Chapter 3, we will dive into the fundamental aspects of flag football. Understanding team composition, player positions, and the core principles of the game is essential for success on the field.

3.1   Team Composition and Player Positions

A well-structured team with players who understand their roles and positions is a recipe for success in flag football. Let's explore this in more detail:

❖ **Understanding Player Roles:** Each player on a flag football team has a specific role and responsibility. These roles are crucial for the team's overall strategy. The quarterback, for instance, is often considered the offense's leader. They call plays, make throws, and direct the team. Wide receivers catch passes and gain yards while running backs focus on carrying the ball and evading defenders. On the defensive side, defensive backs guard receivers and make flag pulls, while rushers aim to pressure the quarterback and disrupt plays. Understanding these roles helps players know where they fit into the team's strategy and how to contribute effectively.

❖ **Importance of Teamwork:** Teamwork is the cornerstone of flag football success. It's about individual skills and how players work together as a cohesive unit. Players must communicate effectively on the field, whether it's the quarterback directing the offense, receivers running precise routes, or defenders coordinating to stop the opposing team. Successful flag football teams often practice plays, refine their timing, and build chemistry to maximize performance.

❖ **Building a Cohesive Unit:** Building team cohesion is a priority for any flag football team. Coaches and team managers play a crucial role in fostering a sense of unity and trust among players. Team-building exercises, both on and off the field, can help players bond and understand each other's strengths and weaknesses. Effective communication is also essential, with clear communication channels between players, coaches, and team leadership. When players trust their teammates and work together seamlessly, it greatly enhances their chances of success.

3.2 Game Fundamentals

Understanding the fundamental aspects of the game is essential for players to perform at their best. Let's delve deeper into these core principles:

❖ **Primary Objective:** Flag football aims to score points by advancing the ball into the opponent's end zone. This straightforward goal guides all offensive strategies and playcalling. Players need to know this objective, as it dictates their actions on the field.

❖ **Scoring Rules:** Flag football scores are achieved through touchdowns, conversions, and field goals. Touchdowns are the most significant scoring plays, worth six points each. Conversions, which follow touchdowns, allow teams to earn additional points, typically one or two, depending on the distance from the goal line. Though less common in flag football than in tackle football, field goals provide three points when successfully executed. Understanding how these scoring mechanisms work is crucial for offensive strategies and point differentials.

❖ **Timing Regulations:** Flag football games have specific time regulations, including quarters or halves. Players need to manage the game clock effectively when they are trailing and conserve time for potential comebacks. Additionally, understanding the play clock is crucial for executing plays efficiently and avoiding penalties. Overtime rules are also essential to grasp, as they can determine the outcome of tied games.

❖ **Starting and Restarting Plays:** Knowing how plays start and restart is fundamental for executing offensive and defensive strategies. The center snap, where the center hikes the ball to the quarterback, initiates most offensive plays.

Defensive players must be aware of the snap count to time their rushes effectively. Restarting plays after stoppages, such as timeouts or penalties, requires precision to regain momentum and capitalize on opportunities.

By grasping these fundamentals, players can develop a strong foundation for success in flag football. Effective teamwork, understanding player roles, and a clear focus on the primary objective of scoring points are the keys to victory. In the upcoming chapters, we will delve deeper into offensive and defensive strategies, advanced techniques, and the mental aspects of flag football, providing the knowledge and skills needed to excel in this exciting sport.

CHAPTER 4
Teamwork and Communication

Chapter 4 will delve into the vital aspects of teamwork and effective communication in flag football. These elements are fundamental to success on the field and contribute to a positive and cohesive team dynamic.

4.1 The Role of Teamwork

Teamwork is the heartbeat of flag football, driving every successful play and fostering a sense of unity among players. Let's explore the critical role of teamwork and its numerous benefits:

❖ **Recognizing Critical Role:** In flag football, individual talent is undoubtedly valuable, but the synergy of the team truly makes a difference. Teamwork isn't merely about passing the ball efficiently or pulling flags with precision; it's about understanding your teammates, anticipating their actions, and creating opportunities for one another. When a team operates as a well-oiled machine, it becomes a formidable force on the field.

❖ **Benefits of Collaborative Play:** Collaborative play in flag football offers many advantages. Firstly, it maximizes each player's strengths. For example, agile receivers who run precise routes can exploit a quarterback's accurate passing. Secondly, teamwork allows for adaptability. Teams can adjust their strategies in response to the opposing team's tactics or changing game situations. Lastly, it enables the execution of complex offensive and defensive plays that require precise timing and coordination. In essence, teamwork amplifies individual abilities and enhances overall team performance.

4.2   Effective Communication

Effective communication is the glue that holds a flag football team together. It's about more than just talking but conveying information clearly and efficiently. Here's a closer look at communication skills and strategies:

❖ **Developing Communication Skills:** On the field, effective communication involves a blend of verbal and non-verbal cues. Verbal communication includes calling plays, indicating routes, or providing feedback to teammates. Non-verbal communication encompasses gestures, eye contact, and body language. Players must practice and refine their communication skills to ensure that everyone conveys messages accurately and understands them.

❖ **On-Field Coordination:** Flag football relies heavily on communication for on-field coordination. Offensive players must signal their routes to the quarterback, who must relay the play to the team efficiently. Defensive players communicate to ensure they cover their assigned zones and coordinate flag pulls. Everyone should be aware of the play's timing and execution. Effective communication is the linchpin that enables these intricate movements to happen smoothly.

❖ **Building Strong Team Bonds:** Effective communication extends beyond the field and is deeply rooted in player relationships. Teams with solid bonds off the field often communicate better on it. Players should engage in team- building activities, spend time together outside practice, and foster trust. In a cohesive and supportive team environment, communication becomes more efficient as players become attuned to each other's tendencies and expectations.

4.3 Leadership and Coaching

Leadership and coaching are integral components of flag football that help cultivate teamwork:

❖ **Exploring Coach's Role:** Coaches and team managers play pivotal roles in nurturing teamwork. They provide guidance, develop strategies, and serve as mentors to players. Coaches ensure that players understand their roles and responsibilities, fostering a sense of unity and purpose. By creating an environment that encourages collaboration and teamwork, coaches set the tone for the entire team.

❖ **Team Managers:** Team managers contribute significantly to team dynamics. They handle administrative tasks, logistics, and player support. A well-organized team manager allows coaches and players to focus more on the game and less on administrative details, fostering a smoother team experience.

23

❖ **Leadership on the Field:** Leadership isn't restricted to coaches and team managers. On the field, players can emerge as leaders by leading by example. This involves demonstrating dedication, commitment, and a strong work ethic. Encouraging and motivating teammates, particularly during challenging moments, is another hallmark of on-field leadership. Leaders help maintain team morale and keep the focus on working together to achieve common goals.

Understanding the pivotal role of teamwork, honing effective communication skills, and recognizing the significance of leadership and coaching are essential aspects of success in flag football. These elements create a positive and cohesive team environment that leads to victories on the field and fosters personal growth and an enjoyable playing experience for all team members.

In the upcoming chapters, we will delve into advanced strategies, mental toughness, and sportsmanship, providing players with the tools they need to excel in flag football.

CHAPTER 5
Mental Toughness and Sportsmanship

Chapter 5 will explore two essential aspects of flag football: mental toughness and sportsmanship. These qualities are crucial for players to not only perform at their best but also contribute positively to the spirit of the game.

5.1   Mental Resilience

Mental resilience is the ability to remain strong and focused, especially in challenging or high-pressure situations. In flag football, where split-second decisions and precise execution are vital, mental toughness can distinguish between success and failure. Here's an in-depth look at mental resilience:

❖ **Developing Mental Toughness:** Mental toughness is a skill that can be cultivated. Players can train their minds to stay calm, focused, and resilient even when facing adversity. Techniques like visualization, mindfulness, and positive self-talk can help players develop mental fortitude.

❖ **Handling Pressure Situations:** Flag football often involves intense moments, whether a critical play, a close game, or the pressure of a crucial match. Players must learn to manage their nerves and maintain composure under pressure. Strategies for staying focused, making sound decisions, and executing plays will be discussed.

❖ **Maintaining Focus:** Concentration is vital in flag football. Distractions can disrupt the flow of the game and lead to mistakes. Players will learn strategies for maintaining an unwavering focus on the task, whether running a route, defending an opponent, or making a crucial flag pull.

❖ **Composure During Games:** Emotions can run high in flag football, particularly in competitive situations. Players will explore methods for staying composed and avoiding emotional reactions that can lead to penalties or poor performance. Maintaining a level head is essential for making rational decisions on the field.

5.2 Sportsmanship and Fair Play

Sportsmanship and fair play are core principles of flag football that extend beyond the game itself. These qualities define the character of players and contribute to a positive playing environment:

❖ **Emphasizing Good Sportsmanship:** Good sportsmanship involves treating opponents, teammates, coaches, and officials with respect and dignity. Players will understand the importance of fair play, adhering to the rules, and exhibiting integrity in all aspects of the game.

❖ **Handling Victories Gracefully:** Celebrating victories is natural, but players will learn to do so gracefully, respecting their opponents and acknowledging their efforts. Gloating

26

or taunting is discouraged, as it goes against the principles of sportsmanship.

- ❖ **Dealing with Losses Gracefully:** Losses are a part of any sport, and players must learn to accept defeat with grace and humility. We'll discuss strategies for handling losses constructively, learning from them, and using them to motivate improvement.

- ❖ **Respecting Officials and Opponents:** Officials and opponents deserve respect, regardless of the game's outcome. Players will be reminded of the importance of treating everyone in the sport courteously and fairly, even in the heat of competition.

Sportsmanship and fair play are not just ideals but fundamental values that should guide every flag football player's conduct. Upholding these principles not only fosters a positive playing environment but also enhances the reputation of the sport and the character of those who participate.

By developing mental resilience and embracing the principles of sportsmanship and fair play, flag football players not only elevate their performance but also contribute positively to the game's overall experience.

The upcoming chapters will explore training and conditioning, offensive and defensive strategies, and advanced techniques to enhance your flag football skills and knowledge.

CHAPTER 6
Training and Conditioning

Chapter 6 focuses on the physical aspects of flag football, emphasizing the importance of proper training, conditioning, and injury prevention. These elements are essential for ensuring that players are physically prepared and can perform at their best on the field.

6.1   Physical Preparation

Flag football is a physically demanding sport that requires players to be in peak condition. Proper physical preparation is crucial for success on the field:

❖ **Preparing with Strength and Agility Workouts:** Strength and agility are essential attributes for flag football players. Strength workouts can help players build the necessary muscle power for activities like passing, receiving, and flag-pulling. Agility training enhances players' ability to change direction quickly, evade defenders, and make sharp cuts during plays. Specific exercises targeting these aspects of fitness, such as weightlifting, sprint drills, and agility ladder exercises, will be covered. Tailoring workouts to individual positions, whether you're a quarterback, receiver, or defender, is vital to optimize performance.

Strength and agility are fundamental aspects of flag football performance. Players need strength for powerful throws, sharp cuts, and flag-pulling, while agility is crucial for evading defenders and making quick directional changes. Tailoring your workouts to your specific position can optimize your performance on the field. Here's a comprehensive guide on strength and agility training for flag football:

Strength Workouts:
Full-Body Strength:
- ✓ **Deadlifts:** Deadlifts build lower body and back strength, which is essential for explosive movements.
- ✓ **Bench Press:** Bench presses strengthen the chest and upper body, aiding in passing and blocking.
- ✓ **Squats:** Squats enhance leg strength, which is critical for running, jumping, and explosive plays.

Upper Body Strength:
- ✓ **Push-Ups:** An effective bodyweight exercise for building chest and triceps strength.
- ✓ **Pull-Ups:** Strengthen the back and biceps, helping with flag-pulling and tackling.
- ✓ **Dumbbell Rows:** Target the upper back and shoulders for improved throwing and catching abilities.

Core Strength:
- ✓ **Planks:** Planks strengthen the core, providing stability and balance on the field.
- ✓ **Russian Twists:** Enhance rotational core strength, crucial for agility and quick directional changes.

✓ **Medicine Ball Throws:** Improve explosive core power for throwing and tackling.

Agility Ladder Drills:

✓ **High Knees:** Enhance leg speed and coordination by running high knees through ladder rungs.

✓ **In-and-Outs:** Work on quick footwork by stepping in and out of ladder squares.

Cone Drills:

✓ **3-Cone Drill:** Set up cones in a triangle formation and practice quick direction changes while running around them.

✓ **Figure 8 Drill:** Arrange cones in a figure-eight pattern and weave through them, improving agility and balance.

Speed and Sprint Drills:

✓ **40-Yard Dash:** Practice sprinting to enhance your speed off the line of scrimmage and when chasing opponents.

✓ **Fartlek Training:** Incorporate interval training with varied sprint distances and rest intervals to simulate game situations.

Reaction Drills:

✓ **Mirror Drills:** Pair up with a teammate and take turns mimicking each other's movements, improving reaction time and mirroring your opponent's actions.

✓ **Ball Reaction Drills:** Practice reacting to a thrown ball by quickly changing direction and adjusting your position to make a play.

Position-Specific Training:
✓ **Quarterbacks:** Focus on arm strength and accuracy through targeted throwing drills. Additionally, agility drills can help with evading pass rushers.
✓ **Receivers:** Prioritize speed, agility, and catching drills to make sharp cuts and secure passes.
✓ **Defenders:** Emphasize flag-pulling drills, agility, and tackling techniques to excel in defensive situations.

Remember to incorporate a balanced training routine that includes both strength and agility workouts. Regular practice and conditioning sessions will help you build the physical attributes necessary to excel in flag football, regardless of your position on the field.

❖ **The Role of Nutrition:** Nutrition is the fuel that powers the body for athletic performance. Players will gain insights into crafting a balanced diet that provides the energy and nutrients needed for peak performance. This includes understanding macronutrients (carbohydrates, proteins, and fats), micronutrients (vitamins and minerals), and the timing of meals for optimal energy levels. Staying well- hydrated is emphasized, as dehydration can impair performance and increase the risk of injury. Players will also learn about pre-game meals that provide sustained energy and post-game nutrition for recovery.

The Role of Nutrition in Flag Football:

Nutrition is a critical factor in ensuring that flag football players perform at their best. A well-balanced diet provides the necessary fuel for energy, supports muscle recovery, and helps players stay hydrated. Here's a comprehensive overview of the role of nutrition in flag football:

1. **Macronutrients:**
   - ✓ Carbohydrates: Carbohydrates are the primary source of energy for athletes. Players should consume complex carbohydrates such as whole grains, fruits, and vegetables to maintain energy levels during practices and games.
   - ✓ Proteins: Protein is essential for muscle repair and growth. Include lean sources of protein like poultry, fish, lean meats, beans, and dairy in your diet to support recovery.
   - ✓ Fats: Healthy fats are important for overall health and can be a source of sustained energy. Incorporate sources like avocados, nuts, seeds, and olive oil into your meals.

2. **Micronutrients:**
   - ✓ Vitamins: A balanced diet rich in fruits and vegetables provides essential vitamins, such as vitamin C and vitamin A, which support the immune system and overall health.

33

✓ Minerals: Minerals like calcium, potassium, and magnesium are crucial for muscle function, hydration, and bone health. Dairy products, leafy greens, and nuts are good sources of these minerals.

3. **Hydration:**
    ✓ Staying well-hydrated is paramount in flag football. Dehydration can lead to decreased performance, muscle cramps, and an increased risk of injury. Players should drink water regularly throughout practices and games.
    ✓ Electrolytes, such as sodium and potassium, are lost through sweat. Consider sports drinks or electrolyte supplements when playing in hot conditions to maintain electrolyte balance.

4. **Timing of Meals:**
    ✓ Pre-Game Meals: Consume a balanced meal 2-3 hours before a game. This meal should be rich in carbohydrates for sustained energy. Avoid heavy, high-fat meals that can cause digestive discomfort.
    ✓ Snacks: A light snack 30 minutes to an hour before the game can provide a quick energy boost. Opt for easily digestible options like a banana, yogurt, or a granola bar.
    ✓ Post-Game Nutrition: After the game, focus on replenishing carbohydrates and proteins to support muscle recovery. Chocolate milk, a turkey sandwich, or a protein shake can be effective choices.

5.   **Recovery:**
   ✓ Proper nutrition post-game is crucial for recovery. Adequate protein intake helps repair muscle tissue. Carbohydrates replenish glycogen stores, while fluids and electrolytes aid in rehydration.
   ✓ Incorporate foods like lean meats, fish, quinoa, and vegetables into your post-game meals to ensure a balanced nutrient intake.

6.   **Avoiding Overconsumption:**
   ✓ Be mindful of portion sizes to avoid Overconsumption of calories. Excess body weight can affect agility and speed on the field.

7.   **Individual Needs:**
   ✓ Nutrition requirements can vary from person to person. Consult with a sports nutritionist or dietitian to create a personalized nutrition plan that aligns with your goals and dietary preferences.

By understanding the role of nutrition and making informed food choices, flag football players can optimize their energy levels, enhance performance, and support overall health. Proper nutrition complements physical training and is a key component of success on the field.

❖ Recovery Strategies: Recovery is an of t e n underestimated aspect of training and conditioning. Proper recovery techniques are essential to prevent overuse injuries and optimize performance. Players will explore strategies for cooling down after practices or games, including stretching routines that promote flexibility and reduce muscle soreness. Adequate rest and sleep play a crucial role in recovery, allowing muscles and the nervous system to recuperate. We'll discuss how players can establish healthy sleep patterns to support their athletic endeavors.

Crucial to flag football player performance is the implementation of proper recovery strategies. These strategies are often underestimated but play a pivotal role in maintaining players' physical and mental well-being, preventing injuries, and optimizing performance on the field. Let's delve deeper into each of these recovery strategies:

1. **Cooling Down and Stretching:**
   ✓ Cooling Down: After a strenuous practice or game, a gradual cool-down is essential. This helps the body transition from intense physical activity to a state of rest, preventing the pooling of blood in the extremities and promoting the removal of metabolic waste products.
   ✓ Stretching: Incorporate stretching routines that focus on flexibility and muscle relaxation. Dynamic stretching, which involves controlled movements, can help improve the range of motion and reduce the risk of injury.

Static stretching, where you hold positions to stretch muscles, is effective for reducing muscle soreness post-activity. Foam rolling, a form of self-myofascial release, can also alleviate muscle tightness and trigger points.

2. **Rest and Sleep:**
   ✓ Adequate Rest: Ensuring you get sufficient rest between practices and games is vital. The body needs time to recover, repair damaged tissues, and replenish energy stores.
   ✓ Quality Sleep: Sleep plays a crucial role in recovery. During sleep, the body undergoes various processes, including hormone regulation and muscle repair. Aim for 7-9 hours of quality sleep per night and establish a consistent sleep schedule to support your athletic endeavors.

3. **Hydration and Nutrition:**
   ✓ Hydration: Proper hydration is critical for recovery. Dehydration can lead to muscle cramps and hinder performance. Replenish fluids lost during activities by drinking water or electrolyte-rich sports drinks when needed.
   ✓ Nutrition: After practices and games, prioritize post-exercise nutrition. Consume a balanced meal or snack that includes carbohydrates to replenish glycogen stores and protein to aid in muscle repair. This can expedite recovery and reduce muscle soreness.

4. **Active Recovery:**
   ✓ Active Rest Days: On rest days, consider engaging in low- intensity activities like walking, swimming, or cycling. Active recovery promotes blood circulation, reducing muscle stiffness and aiding overall recovery.

5. **Listen to Your Body:**
   ✓ Self-Assessment: Pay attention to your body's signals. If you experience persistent soreness, fatigue, or discomfort, it's crucial to respect these signals and allow your body the time it needs to recover fully. Overtraining can lead to burnout and an increased risk of injuries.

6. **Injury Management:**
   ✓ Professional Guidance: In the event of an injury, seek appropriate medical attention. Follow the rehabilitation plan prescribed by healthcare professionals to ensure a safe and efficient recovery process.

7. **Mental Recovery:**
   ✓ Mental Fatigue: Mental recovery is just as essential as physical recovery. Practices like mindfulness, meditation, or relaxation techniques can help reduce stress, improve mental clarity, and enhance overall well-being.

8. **Recovery Tools:**
   ✓ Utilize Resources: Consider using recovery tools like ice baths, compression garments, or massage therapy. These tools can help reduce inflammation, alleviate muscle soreness, and accelerate the recovery process.

9. **Periodization:**
   - ✓ Structured Training: Implement a periodization plan in your training program. Periodization involves structured training phases with varying intensity and volume. It prevents burnout, minimizes the risk of overtraining, and allows for optimal recovery between training sessions.

10. **Cross-Training:**
    - ✓ Diversify Training: Cross-training in other sports or activities can be beneficial. It reduces the repetitive stress on specific muscle groups, enhances overall fitness, and lowers the risk of overuse injuries.

11. **Professional Guidance:**
    - ✓ Consult Experts: Seek guidance from sports therapists, physical therapists, or certified trainers. They can provide personalized advice on recovery techniques, injury prevention, and tailored training programs.

Incorporating these comprehensive recovery strategies into your flag football routine not only safeguards your physical health but also ensures you're consistently at your best on the field, ready to perform at your highest potential. Prioritizing recovery is a key component of long-term success in flag football.

6.2 Injury Prevention

In flag football, as in any sport, injuries can occur. However, players can take proactive measures to reduce the risk of injuries and respond effectively when they happen:

❖ Prioritizing Injury Prevention: Prevention starts with proper warm-up exercises to prepare the body for physical activity. Players will learn about dynamic warm-up routines that enhance blood flow, improve flexibility, and reduce the risk of strains and sprains. Staying hydrated is emphasized, as dehydration can lead to muscle cramps and heat-related issues. Players will also understand the importance of staying well-hydrated to prevent injuries.

Prioritizing Injury Prevention in Flag Football:
Injury prevention is a critical aspect of flag football, as it not only keeps players safe but also ensures their ability to perform at their best. Here are key injury prevention strategies for flag football players:

1. **Dynamic Warm-Up:**
   ✓ Importance of Warm-Up: Proper warm-up exercises are essential to prepare the body for physical activity. They increase blood flow, improve muscle flexibility, and enhance joint mobility, reducing the risk of strains, sprains, and other injuries.
   ✓ Dynamic Warm-Up Routines: Players should incorporate dynamic warm-up routines that involve active movements like leg swings, arm circles, high knees, and

butt kicks. These exercises help activate muscles, lubricate joints, and mentally prepare for the game.

2. **Hydration:**
   - ✓ Prevent Dehydration: Staying hydrated is crucial to prevent injuries. Dehydration can lead to muscle cramps, fatigue, and an increased risk of heat-related issues. Ensure you drink water regularly before, during, and after practices and games.
   - ✓ Electrolytes: In hot conditions or during intense physical activity, consider consuming sports drinks or electrolyte supplements to maintain electrolyte balance and prevent cramping.

3. **Proper Conditioning:**
   - ✓ Strength and Conditioning: A well-rounded strength and conditioning program can improve muscular strength, endurance, and overall fitness. Strong muscles and good cardiovascular conditioning reduce the risk of injuries.
   - ✓ Functional Training: Incorporate functional exercises that mimic movements and demands specific to flag football. Focus on exercises that target the muscles and joints involved in flag-pulling, passing, and running.

4. **Safe Tackling Techniques:**
   - ✓ Flag-pulling: Flag-pulling is a fundamental defensive skill in flag football. Players should learn and practice safe flag- pulling techniques to avoid unnecessary contact and potential injuries.

5. **Adequate Rest and Recovery:**
   ✓ Rest Between Practices: Ensure you have sufficient rest between practices and games to allow your body to recover. Overtraining increases the risk of injuries due to fatigue and reduced muscle performance.

6. **Protective Gear:**
   ✓ Appropriate Attire: Wear appropriate attire and footwear for flag football. This includes non-slip shoes with good traction and comfortable clothing that doesn't restrict movement.
   ✓ Mouthguards: While not mandatory in flag football, wearing a mouthguard can protect against dental injuries.

7. **Injury Recognition and Reporting:**
   ✓ Awareness: Players should be aware of the signs of potential injuries, such as strains, sprains, or concussions. If you suspect an injury, report it to your coach or medical staff promptly.

8. **Proper Coaching:**
   ✓ Coaching Education: Coaches should be knowledgeable about injury prevention and safe training practices. They should also emphasize the importance of proper technique to minimize injury risks.

9. **Field Conditions:**
   ✓ Inspect the Field: Before practices or games, players and coaches should inspect the field for any hazards or irregularities, such as holes or obstacles, that could cause tripping or falling.

10. **Communication:**
    - ✓ Open Communication: Players should communicate openly with coaches and teammates about any discomfort or pain they may experience. Early intervention can prevent minor issues from becoming more serious injuries.

Prioritizing injury prevention through these strategies helps flag football players stay safe and enjoy the sport to the fullest. By taking proactive steps to reduce injury risks, players can maintain their physical well-being and continue to excel on the field.

❖ **Understanding Common Injuries:** While flag football doesn't involve full-contact tackles, players can still experience injuries. Understanding the nature of these injuries is essential for prevention and early intervention. Common flag football injuries include ankle sprains, hamstring strains, and minor contusions. Players will learn to recognize the signs and symptoms of these injuries and take precautions to minimize their risk.

Let's delve deeper into the understanding of common injuries in flag football, their nature, prevention, and how to manage them:

1. **Ankle Sprains:**
    - ✓ Nature of Injury: Ankle sprains are one of the most prevalent injuries in flag football. They typically occur when the ligaments surrounding the ankle joint are

stretched or torn due to an abrupt change in direction or a landing on an uneven surface.

✓ Signs and Symptoms: Ankle sprains are characterized by pain, swelling, bruising, and sometimes a popping sound at the time of injury. Players may find it challenging to put weight on the affected ankle.

✓ Prevention: To prevent ankle sprains, players should wear well-fitted athletic shoes that provide ankle support. Regular ankle-strengthening exercises and balance training can help increase stability and reduce the risk of sprains. Being cautious during sudden directional changes and maintaining proper field conditions are also preventive measures.

2. **Hamstring Strains:**
    ✓ Nature of Injury: Hamstring strains are injuries to the muscles and tendons at the back of the thigh. They often occur during sprinting, quick acceleration, or deceleration when the hamstring muscles are stretched beyond their capacity.

    ✓ Signs and Symptoms: Hamstring strains typically manifest as a sudden sharp pain in the back of the thigh. There may be tenderness, swelling, and difficulty extending the leg.

    ✓ Prevention: Proper warm-up routines that include dynamic stretching of the hamstring muscles are crucial for prevention. Strength training exercises targeting the hamstrings can also help reduce the risk of strains. En-

suring that players are adequately conditioned and grad-
ually increasing intensity during training can further
lower the risk.

✓

3. **Minor Contusions (Bruises):**
   ✓ Nature of Injury: Contusions or bruises result from
   blunt trauma or impact. In flag football, they can occur
   when players collide with opponents or the ground.
   ✓ Signs and Symptoms: Contusions are identified by localized pain, swelling, and discoloration (bruising) at
   the site of impact.
   ✓ Prevention: While it's challenging to completely prevent contusions in a contact sport, players can reduce
   their risk by wearing protective gear, such as padded
   clothing or compression sleeves. Ensuring fair play and
   adhering to flag-pulling rules can also minimize the
   likelihood of collisions.

4. **Minor Cuts and Abrasions:**
   ✓ Nature of Injury: Minor cuts and abrasions are surface
   wounds that happen when players come into contact
   with abrasive surfaces, like the playing field or other
   players' equipment.
   ✓ Signs and Symptoms: These injuries are marked by
   open wounds, pain, and sometimes bleeding.
   ✓ Prevention: Players can prevent minor cuts and abrasions by wearing appropriate clothing with long sleeves

and pants. Adequate hygiene, cleaning, and applying antiseptic to wounds can help prevent infection.

5. **Minor Sprains and Strains:**
   ✓ Nature of Injury: Minor sprains and strains can affect various muscle groups and result from sudden movements, twists, or overexertion.
   ✓ Signs and Symptoms: These injuries typically involve localized pain, swelling, and limited range of motion.
   ✓ Prevention: Maintaining overall physical conditioning through flexibility and strength training can lower the risk of minor sprains and strains. Adequate warm-up and cooldown routines before and after play can also help minimize these injuries.

Understanding these common injuries and taking proactive measures to prevent them is essential for flag football players and coaches. By prioritizing injury prevention through proper conditioning, warm-up routines, protective gear, and fair play, players can enjoy a safer and more enjoyable flag football experience.

❖ **Basic First Aid Techniques:** In flag football, players should have a basic understanding of first aid techniques to address minor injuries promptly. This includes knowing how to apply ice to reduce swelling, bandage minor wounds to prevent infection, and provide initial care until more comprehensive medical attention is available. Players will recognize the importance of safety on the field and taking care of themselves and their teammates.

Basic First Aid Techniques in Flag Football:

In flag football, it's essential for players to have a basic understanding of first aid techniques to address minor injuries promptly and ensure the well-being of themselves and their teammates. Here are some fundamental first-aid techniques:

1. **Applying Ice for Swelling:**
   - ✓ Nature of Injury: Ice is commonly used to reduce swelling and inflammation resulting from minor injuries like sprains, strains, or contusions.
   - ✓ First Aid Technique:
   - ✓ Place crushed ice or an ice pack in a clean cloth or plastic bag.
   - ✓ Apply the ice to the injured area for 15-20 minutes at a time, with breaks in between.
   - ✓ Ensure there's a barrier (cloth or plastic) between the ice and the skin to prevent frostbite.

2. **Bandaging Minor Wounds:**
   - ✓ Nature of Injury: In flag football, players may sustain minor cuts, scrapes, or abrasions that require immediate attention to prevent infection.
   - ✓ First Aid Technique:
   - ✓ Wash your hands with soap and water, or use hand sanitizer.
   - ✓ Clean the wound gently with mild soap and water.

47

✓ Apply an over-the-counter antibiotic ointment to the wound.

✓ Cover the wound with a sterile adhesive bandage or dressing.

✓ Replace the bandage as needed to keep the wound clean and dry.

3. **Treating Minor Burns:**

✓ Nature of Injury: Minor burns can occur if a player comes into contact with hot surfaces, equipment, or friction with the ground.

✓ First Aid Technique:

✓ For minor burns, cool the affected area with cold running water for 10-20 minutes to reduce pain and prevent further damage.

✓ Apply a sterile, non-stick dressing or clean cloth to the burn.

4. **Managing Sprains and Strains:**

✓ Nature of Injury: Sprains and strains can happen during flag football, and players should know how to provide initial care.

✓ First Aid Technique:

✓ For sprains and strains, use the R.I.C.E. method:

✓ Rest: Encourage the injured player to rest and avoid putting weight on the injured area.

✓ Ice: Apply ice to reduce swelling (as described above).

✓ Compression: Use an elastic bandage to compress the injured area gently to limit swelling.

✓ Elevation: Elevate the injured limb above the level of the heart when possible to reduce swelling.

5. **Recognizing the Importance of Safety:**

✓ Players should also recognize the importance of safety on the field and encourage their teammates to play responsibly and within the rules of the game.

✓ If a player sustains a potentially serious injury, such as a head injury, neck injury, or suspected fracture, it's crucial to immobilize the injured player and seek immediate medical assistance. Do not attempt to move the injured player unless it's absolutely necessary for their safety.

While these basic first-aid techniques can address minor injuries in flag football, it's important to remember that more serious injuries may require professional medical attention. Players and coaches should prioritize safety on the field, encourage fair play, and have a designated person trained in first aid available during practices and games to handle injuries appropriately.

Physical preparation and injury prevention are intertwined aspects of flag football that ensure players are not only in top physical condition but also safeguarded against injuries that can sideline them. By dedicating themselves to proper training, nutrition, and recovery, players can maximize their potential on the field while minimizing the risk of setbacks. In the upcoming chapters, we will delve into offensive and defensive strategies, advanced techniques, and the path to building a future in flag football, including college and scholarship opportunities.

CHAPTER 7
Offensive Strategies

7.1   Building an Offensive Playbook

Building an offensive playbook is like crafting a winning strategy that guides your team to success on the flag football field. Here's a more detailed look at the essential components of an offensive playbook:

❖ **Developing Offensive Strategies:** Effective offensive strategies are born from a deep understanding of your team's strengths, weaknesses, and unique player attributes. It's essential to assess your team's composition, including the skills and attributes of each player. For example, if you have a quarterback with great accuracy and a strong arm, your playbook might lean toward passing plays. Conversely, if your team has speedy and agile receivers, shorter, quicker passing plays may be your forte. Tailoring your playbook to maximize your team's potential and exploit your opponents' weaknesses is fundamental.

Developing Effective Offensive Strategies in Flag Football: Creating successful offensive strategies in flag football requires a thorough understanding of your team's capabilities and a tailored approach to exploit opponents' weaknesses. Here's a step-by-step guide on how to develop and implement offensive strategies:

1. **Assess Your Team's Composition:**
   - ✓ Skills and Attributes: Evaluate your team's strengths and weaknesses. Consider the skills and attributes of each player, including their speed, agility, passing ability, catching skills, and flag-pulling capabilities.
   - ✓ Player Roles: Identify key roles within your team, such as the quarterback, receivers, and rusher, and assess their strengths and limitations.

2. **Define Your Playbook:**
   - ✓ Passing vs. Running: Decide whether your team's strengths lean more towards passing or running plays. This decision should be based on the assessment of your players' skills.
   - ✓ Diversity of Plays: Develop a diverse playbook that includes a variety of passing and running plays. Having multiple options keeps the defense guessing and enhances your team's versatility.
   - ✓ Specialized Plays: Consider incorporating specialized plays, trick plays, and unique formations that can catch opponents off guard. These can include double passes, laterals, and misdirection plays.

3. **Study Opponents:**
   - ✓ Scouting: Research and analyze your opponents' defensive strategies and tendencies. Identify weaknesses in their defense that your team can exploit.

✓ Player Matchups: Pay attention to player matchups. If you have a receiver with a speed advantage over a defender, plan plays that capitalize on this mismatch.

4. **Create Game Plans:**

✓ Tailored Approach: Customize your game plans based on the strengths and weaknesses of your opponents. Develop specific strategies for each game to maximize your chances of success.

✓ Situational Awareness: Consider situational factors, such as the score, time remaining, and field position, when developing game plans. Adjust your strategies accordingly.

5. **Emphasize Communication and Timing:**

✓ On-Field Communication: Encourage effective communication between players on the field. Clear and concise signals and calls can help execute plays smoothly.

✓ Timing: Timing is crucial in flag football. Quarterbacks must establish a rapport with their receivers to ensure well-timed throws and routes. Practice timing drills to improve coordination.

6. **Practice and Repetition:**

✓ Drills: Consistent practice and drill work are essential for improving offensive execution. This includes running passing routes, working on quarterback-receiver timing, and perfecting blocking techniques.

✓ Scrimmages: Organize scrimmages and simulated game situations to practice offensive plays in a game-like setting.

7. **Adapt and Adjust:**
   - ✓ In-Game Adaptation: Be prepared to adapt your offensive strategies during games based on how the opponent reacts. If a certain play or approach isn't working, make adjustments.

8. **Team Cohesion:**
   - ✓ Building Team Chemistry: Foster team cohesion and chemistry to enhance trust and understanding among players. A well-knit team can execute offensive plays more effectively.

9. **Analyze Performance:**
   - ✓ Post-Game Analysis: After each game, analyze your offensive performance. Identify what worked well and what needs improvement. Use this feedback to refine your strategies for future games.

10. **Continual Learning:**
   - ✓ Stay Informed: Keep up with the latest trends and innovations in flag football strategies. Attend workshops, watch professional games, and seek input from experienced coaches and players.

Developing effective offensive strategies in flag football is an ongoing process that combines careful planning, adaptability, and teamwork. By tailoring your playbook to your team's strengths, analyzing opponents, and continually refining your approach, you can enhance your chances of offensive success on the field.

❖ **Maximizing Scoring Opportunities:** The primary objective of your offensive strategies is to create scoring opportunities and convert them into points. This involves a deep understanding of defensive coverages, recognizing open spaces on the field, and exploiting defensive vulnerabilities. You'll delve into various tactics and plays that help your team advance the ball effectively and efficiently towards the end zone. A well-balanced offense that mixes running and passing plays keeps the defense guessing and adds versatility to your game.

Maximizing Scoring Opportunities in Flag Football:
Scoring is the ultimate goal of any offensive strategy in flag football. To maximize scoring opportunities, your team should focus on a combination of tactics, plays, and teamwork. Here's how to achieve this:

1. **Understanding Defensive Coverages:**
    ✓ Read the Defense: Quarterbacks should develop the ability to read the opposing defense. This includes identifying whether the defense is playing man-to-man coverage, zone coverage, or a combination of both.
    ✓ Exploiting Gaps: Recognize gaps or soft spots in the defense. These are areas where receivers can get open and where the quarterback can deliver accurate passes.

2. **Utilizing Various Tactics and Plays:**
    ✓ Mix of Running and Passing: A balanced offense keeps the defense guessing. Incorporate both running and

passing plays into your playbook to keep opponents off-balance.

✓ Quick Passing Game: Quick, short passes can be effective for gaining yardage and maintaining possession. Quick releases from the quarterback and sharp route-running by receivers are crucial.

✓ Deep Passing Threat: Develop plays that target deep routes to stretch the defense vertically. This forces defenders to cover more ground and can create big-play opportunities.

✓ Screen Plays: Screen passes to running backs or receivers can be effective in creating open-field opportunities. These plays often require good blocking from the offensive line and quick decision- making by the quarterback.

✓ Trick Plays: Incorporate trick plays and misdirections into your playbook to catch the defense off guard. These can include reverses, double passes, and lateral plays.

3.   **Ball Movement and Player Mobility:**

✓ Ball Movement: Keep the ball moving quickly within the offense. This prevents the defense from settling and reacting predictably.

✓ Player Mobility: Encourage receivers to use their speed and agility to create separation from defenders. Sharp cuts, jukes, and changes in direction can help receivers get open.

4.   **Timing and Precision:**

   ✓ Timing: Work on timing between the quarterback and receivers. Well-timed throws and precise routes are essential for successful passing plays.

   ✓ Precision: Emphasize precision in route-running and execution. Mistimed passes or imprecise routes can result in incomplete passes or turnovers.

5.   **Adjustments and Audibles:**

   ✓ In-Game Adjustments: Be prepared to make adjustments during the game based on the defense's reactions. If a particular play or tactic is consistently successful, exploit it. If not, be ready to change the approach.

   ✓ Audibles: Quarterbacks should have the ability to call audibles at the line of scrimmage based on what they see from the defense. This can involve changing the play or route based on the defensive alignment.

6.   **Teamwork and Communication:**

   ✓ Effective Communication: Ensure that players communicate effectively on the field. This includes calling plays, making route adjustments, and providing feedback to one another.

   ✓ Blocking: Good blocking by receivers and offensive linemen can create running lanes and protect the quarterback. Teach players how to block effectively without holding.

Red Zone Strategies:

❖ **Red Zone Efficiency:** Focus on strategies for scoring when your offense enters the red zone (inside the opponent's 20-yard line). Red zone plays often require precise execution due to limited space.

By implementing these strategies and continually refining your offensive approach, your team can maximize scoring opportunities in flag football. Adaptability, precision, and teamwork are key to achieving success on the field and putting points on the scoreboard.

7.2   Passing and Route Running

In flag football, the passing game is often the key to offensive success. Understanding passing and route running is essential for creating a potent offensive attack:

❖ **Understanding Passing Plays:** Passing plays are the backbone of flag football offense. Successful execution relies on quarterbacks' ability to read the defense, identify open receivers, and deliver accurate passes. You'll explore various passing plays, from quick, short throws to deep passes that stretch the field. Strategies for evading the rush, creating passing lanes, and adapting to changing game situations will be discussed. Timing, precision, and a deep understanding of your receivers' routes and defensive coverages are vital for successful passing plays.

❖ **Route Running for a Potent Offense:** Route running is an art form that combines precision, strategy, and athleticism. You'll delve into different route options, such as post routes, slants, and curls, and learn how to use them to exploit defensive coverages. Creating separation from defenders, making sharp cuts, and adjusting routes on the fly are skills that can significantly impact your offensive success. Effective route running is not just about speed; it's about the subtleties of deception and agility.

❖ **Tips for Successful Passes and Receptions:** Successful passing and receiving require a strong connection between quarterbacks and receivers. Quarterbacks will gain valuable tips on making quick decisions, avoiding interceptions, and delivering accurate passes. Receivers will explore catching techniques, including hand positioning, body control, and creating space from defenders. Additionally, securing the flag after receptions is a critical aspect of flag football that will be emphasized.

Mastering offensive strategies, passing, and route running can transform your team into a formidable offensive force. With a well- structured playbook and honed skills, you'll create ample scoring opportunities and contribute significantly to your team's success on the field. In the upcoming chapters, we will dive into defensive strategies, advanced techniques, and the path to building a future in flag football, including college and scholarship opportunities.

1. Building an Offensive Playbook

Building a comprehensive offensive playbook is akin to constructing a strategic roadmap for success on the flag football field. Let's delve deeper into the essential components of an offensive playbook:

❖ **Developing Offensive Strategies**: Effective offensive strategies are rooted in a deep understanding of your team's capabilities and the unique strengths of individual players. It's essential to assess your team's composition, including the skills and attributes of each player. For instance, if you have a strong-armed quarterback, you might emphasize long-passing plays. Alternatively, if your team boasts agile and quick receivers, shorter, more intricate passing plays may be more effective. Tailoring your playbook to maximize your team's potential is the cornerstone of offensive success.

❖ **Maximizing Scoring Opportunities:** The primary objective of any offense is to score points. Effective offensive strategies are designed to exploit the weaknesses in the opposing defense and create scoring opportunities. This involves a deep understanding of defensive coverages, open areas on the field, and exploiting vulnerabilities in the defense's alignment. Developing plays that efficiently advance the ball toward the end zone is crucial. Balancing your offensive approach with both running and passing plays keeps the defense guessing and adds versatility to your playbook.

The passing game is the heartbeat of flag football offense, and mastering the art of passing and route running is essential for a high-powered attack:

❖ **Understanding Passing Plays:** Passing plays are the foundation of flag football offense. Successful execution hinges on quarterbacks' abilities to read the defense, identify open receivers, and deliver accurate passes. Understanding defensive coverages and recognizing potential mismatches are key skills for quarterbacks. Additionally, quarterbacks must have a mastery of timing and ball placement to connect with their targets. Protection from the offensive line and the ability to evade the pass rush are critical aspects of executing passing plays effectively. Strategies for creating passing lanes, utilizing pump fakes, and adjusting to defensive pressure will be explored.

Understanding Passing Plays in Flag Football:

Passing plays are the cornerstone of any effective flag football offense. To excel in this aspect of the game, both quarterbacks and receivers must work in harmony to read the defense, exploit openings, and execute precise passes. Here's a deeper dive into the key components of passing plays in flag football:

1. **Reading the Defense:**
   ✓ Pre-Snap Reads: Before the snap, quarterbacks must assess the defensive alignment, looking for potential weaknesses or mismatches in coverage.

✓ Post-Snap Reads: As the play unfolds, quarterbacks need to read the defense's movements to identify open receivers. This involves recognizing zone versus man-to-man coverage, anticipating defenders' reactions, and making quick decisions.

2.   **Identifying Open Receivers:**
✓ Route Running: Receivers run specific routes designed to get them open. Quarterbacks must trust that their receivers will execute these routes effectively and be in the right place at the right time.
✓ Finding the Soft Spots: Understanding defensive coverages is crucial. Quarterbacks should look for areas of the field where defenders are less likely to be, such as the gaps between zones, to locate open receivers.

3.   **Ball Placement and Timing:**
✓ Accuracy: Accurate passing is essential. Quarterbacks must place the ball where only their receiver can catch it, typically low and away from defenders' reach.
✓ Timing: Timing is everything in flag football passing. Quarterbacks and receivers must be in sync, with the throw released just before the receiver makes their break.

4.   **Offensive Line Protection:**
✓ Pass Blocking: The offensive line plays a pivotal role in protecting the quarterback. They must form a strong

pocket and fend off the pass rush to give the quarterback time to make decisions and set up throws.

✓ Evasion Skills: When pass protection breaks down, quarterbacks must be agile enough to evade the pass rush, whether by stepping up in the pocket or rolling out to buy time.

5. **Creating Passing Lanes:**

✓ Moving in the Pocket: Quarterbacks should move within the pocket to create passing lanes. This involves stepping forward, backward, or sideways to get a better view of the field.

✓ Using Pump Fakes: Employing pump fakes can help freeze defenders and open up passing lanes. By faking a throw in one direction and then targeting another receiver, quarterbacks can exploit defensive reactions.

6. **Adjusting to Defensive Pressure:**

✓ Quick Decisions: When facing a heavy pass rush, quarterbacks must make quick decisions. This may involve getting rid of the ball to avoid a sack or extending the play to create new opportunities.

✓ Dump-Off Options: Having short, safe passing options as a contingency plan can help mitigate pressure. These quick throws can turn into positive gains when executed effectively.

✓ Route Running for a Potent Offense: Route running is an art form that demands precision, agility, and deception. Receivers must execute crisp routes to gain separation from defenders and provide the quarterback with a clear target. Different routes serve distinct purposes, from quick short- yardage gains to stretching the field vertically. Understanding when and how to run specific routes based on the defensive coverage is a fundamental skill. Receivers will learn techniques for selling their routes through body language, making sharp cuts to elude defenders, and adjusting their routes on the fly to exploit defensive weaknesses.

Route Running Techniques for a Potent Flag Football Offense: Route running is a crucial skill for receivers in flag football. To become effective route runners, players must master a combination of precision, agility, and deception. Here are key elements of route running for a potent offense:

1. **Precision in Route Running:**
    - ✓ Crisp Cuts: Sharp, well-timed cuts are the foundation of successful route running. Receivers must practice making precise cuts to change direction quickly and create separation from defenders.
    - ✓ Consistent Strides: Maintaining consistent stride lengths during routes helps receivers stay balanced and prevents defenders from reading their intentions.
2. **Understanding Route Variations:**
    - ✓ Short Routes (Quick Outs, Slants, Hitches): Short routes are designed for gaining quick yards. Receivers must explode off the line, make a precise cut, and create separation for a brief pass opportunity.

- ✓ Intermediate Routes (Curls, Comebacks, Digs): Intermediate routes involve crisper breaks and require receivers to maintain separation from defenders while creating windows for throws.
- ✓ Deep Routes (Post, Go, Corner): Deep routes aim to stretch the field vertically. Receivers must combine speed and route-running finesse to get behind defenders and give the quarterback a deep target.

3. **Reading Defensive Coverage:**
   - ✓ Zone vs. Man Coverage: Receivers must read the defensive coverage to adjust their routes. In man-to-man coverage, creating separation through sharp cuts and speed is essential. In zone coverage, finding open spots in the zone and sitting down is key.

4. **Selling Routes through Deception:**
   - ✓ Head and Shoulder Fakes: Receivers can use head and shoulder fakes to deceive defenders about their intended route. A subtle fake in one direction followed by a sharp cut in another can leave defenders flat-footed.
   - ✓ Change of Speed: Varying speed during a route can keep defenders guessing. A sudden burst of speed after a fake can help create separation.

5. **Adjusting Routes on the Fly:**
   - ✓ Recognizing Defensive Adjustments: Receivers must be aware of how defenders react to their routes. If a defender takes away the primary route, the receiver should be prepared to adjust and find an alternative open space.

✓ Option Routes: Some routes allow receivers to make decisions based on the defender's positioning. Receivers and quarterbacks must be on the same page to exploit these options effectively.

6. **Non-Verbal Communication:**

✓ Eye Contact: Maintaining eye contact with the quarterback can signal the intention to cut or break. Receivers must establish trust and understanding with their quarterback.

✓ Hand Signals: Non-verbal signals between the quarterback and receivers can communicate adjustments or audibles on the fly.

7. **Practice and Repetition:**

✓ Drill Work: Consistent practice and drill work are essential for improving route running. This includes running routes against defenders, working on timing with the quarterback, and refining cutting techniques.

Practice and repetition are the cornerstones of skill development in flag football. To become a proficient route runner and an asset to the offense, players must engage in regular and focused practice. Here's a closer look at the importance of practice and drill work for improving route running:

1. **Consistency is Key:**

✓ Regular practice sessions are essential for honing route running skills. Consistency helps players build muscle memory and refine their technique over time.

✓ Routinely practicing routes allows players to fine-tune their cuts, timing, and positioning, making them more reliable targets for the quarterback.

2. **Running Routes Against Defenders:**
   ✓ Running routes against defenders in practice replicates game-like scenarios. It helps receivers learn how to create separation when faced with actual defensive coverage.
   ✓ Defenders in practice can provide valuable feedback and challenges, forcing receivers to adapt and improve.

3. **Timing with the Quarterback:**
   ✓ Building chemistry with the quarterback is vital for successful route running. Practicing with the same quarterback allows players to establish trust and timing in their connections.
   ✓ Quarterbacks and receivers should work together to ensure their timing aligns with the specific routes being run. This can include the release point of the ball and the receiver's break on the route.

4. **Refining Cutting Techniques:**
   ✓ Route running involves precise cuts and changes of direction. Repetition of these cuts, such as quick breaks on slants or sharp cuts on comebacks, is essential for improvement.
   ✓ Fine-tuning cutting techniques includes focusing on footwork, balance, and body control. Practicing these elements helps receivers execute sharp and unpredictable cuts.

5. **Drills for Route Running:**
   - ✓ Cone Drills: Set up cones to mark the route and practice making precise cuts around them. This helps with agility and route precision.
   - ✓ Route Tree Drills: Work through a variety of routes from the route tree, including short, intermediate, and deep routes. Focus on executing each route with precision.
   - ✓ Reaction Drills: Use defenders or coaches to simulate game situations. Receivers must react to the defense's movements and adjust their routes accordingly.

6. **Video Analysis:**
   - ✓ Recording practice sessions and reviewing them can provide valuable insights. Players can assess their route running technique, footwork, and timing to identify areas for improvement.
   - ✓ Video analysis also allows coaches to provide targeted feedback and corrections.

7. **Mental Reps:**
   - ✓ Mental visualization of routes and scenarios can complement physical practice. Players can mentally rehearse their routes, reads, and adjustments, which can enhance their on-field performance.

8. **Consistent Feedback:**
   - ✓ Coaches should provide ongoing feedback and corrections during practice sessions. This ensures that players are aware of their strengths and areas for improvement.

✓ Encouraging a growth mindset, where players see challenges as opportunities for growth, can foster a culture of continuous improvement.

By committing to consistent practice and drill work, players can elevate their route running skills, ultimately contributing to a more potent and efficient flag football offense. The combination of physical and mental repetition is essential for achieving mastery in route running and becoming a reliable asset to the team.

By mastering these route-running techniques, receivers can become reliable targets for the quarterback and make the offense more dynamic. Flag football offenses thrive when receivers can gain separation, make quick decisions, and adapt to defensive coverages effectively.

By mastering these aspects of passing plays, quarterbacks and their receiving corps can become a formidable force in flag football. A well-executed passing game can keep defenses guessing, create big plays, and ultimately lead to offensive success on the field.

Tips for Successful Passes and Receptions: Successful passing and receiving rely on the synergy between quarterbacks and receivers. Quarterbacks must develop the ability to read defenses, avoid interceptions, and deliver precise throws. Receivers, on the other hand, need to track the ball effectively, secure catches, and protect the flag after receptions. Tips for quarterbacks on making quick decisions, understanding defensive schemes, and delivering on- target throws will be covered. Receivers will gain insights into catching techniques, including hand positioning, body control, and creating separation from defenders to improve their reception skills.

Understanding Passing Plays in Flag Football:
Passing plays are the backbone of a successful flag football offense. To master this critical aspect of the game, quarterbacks and receivers must work in tandem to read the defense, exploit openings, and execute precise passes. Here's an in-depth look at the key components of passing plays in flag football:

1. **Reading the Defense:**
   - ✓ Pre-Snap Reads: Before the snap, quarterbacks must assess the defensive alignment. They should look for potential weaknesses or mismatches in coverage, including identifying which defenders may be responsible for covering specific receivers.
   - ✓ Post-Snap Reads: As the play unfolds, quarterbacks need to read the defense's movements and reactions. This involves recognizing whether the defense is playing zone or man-to- man coverage, anticipating how defenders will react to the play, and making quick decisions based on those observations.

2.   **Identifying Open Receivers:**
   ✓ Route Running: Receivers run predefined routes designed to create separation from defenders. Quarterbacks must trust that their receivers will execute these routes effectively and be in the right position at the right time.
   ✓ Finding the Soft Spots: Understanding defensive coverages is crucial. Quarterbacks should look for areas of the field where defenders are less likely to be, such as the gaps between zones or behind defenders in man coverage. These "soft spots" are where open receivers can be found.

3.   **Ball Placement and Timing:**
   ✓ Accuracy: Precision passing is paramount. Quarterbacks must place the ball where only their intended receiver can make the catch, typically low and away from defenders' reach.
   ✓ Timing: Timing is the essence of flag football passing. Quarterbacks and receivers must be in sync, with the throw released just before the receiver makes their break. Timing is crucial for completing passes and avoiding interceptions.

4.   **Offensive Line Protection:**
   ✓ Pass Blocking: The offensive line plays a pivotal role in protecting the quarterback. They must create a solid pocket by blocking defenders to give the quarterback time to make decisions and set up their throws.

✓ Evasion Skills: When pass protection breaks down, quarterbacks must demonstrate agility to evade the pass rush. This can involve stepping up in the pocket, side-stepping defenders, or even rolling out to buy additional time.

5. **Creating Passing Lanes:**

✓ Moving in the Pocket: Quarterbacks should move within the pocket to create better passing lanes. This means stepping forward, backward, or sideways to gain a clearer view of the field and find open receivers.

✓ Using Pump Fakes: Employing pump fakes can freeze defenders and open up passing lanes. By faking a throw in one direction and then targeting another receiver, quarterbacks can exploit defensive reactions and create opportunities.

6. **Adjusting to Defensive Pressure:**

✓ Quick Decisions: When facing a heavy pass rush, quarterbacks must make rapid decisions. This may involve quickly releasing the ball to avoid a sack or extending the play to create new passing opportunities.

✓ Dump-Off Options: Having short, safe passing options as a contingency plan can help alleviate pressure. Quick throws to these "dump-off" options can turn into positive gains when executed effectively.

Mastery of passing plays in flag football requires a combination of mental acuity, physical skill, and teamwork between quarterbacks and receivers. By honing these skills and continually practicing and refining passing plays, your team can excel in the passing game and become a formidable offensive force on the field.

A well-crafted offensive playbook, coupled with proficiency in passing and route running, can transform a mediocre flag football team into a formidable offensive powerhouse. By implementing a strategic playbook and mastering the intricacies of passing and receiving, players can create abundant scoring opportunities and consistently outperform their opponents. In the forthcoming chapters, we will delve into defensive strategies, advanced techniques, and the path to building a future in flag football, including college and scholarship opportunities.

CHAPTER 8
Defensive Strategies

In Chapter 8, we will explore the essential elements of defensive strategies in flag football. A strong defense is as vital as a potent offense, and this chapter will equip players with the knowledge and skills needed to excel on the defensive side of the field.

8.1   Creating an Effective Defense

An effective defense is the bedrock of success in flag football. It's essential to understand the intricacies of developing a formidable defensive game plan:

❖ **Developing a Strong Defensive Game Plan:** The first step in creating an effective defense is conducting thorough research on your upcoming opponents. This involves scouting your opponents to identify their strengths, weaknesses, and tendencies. Recognizing key players and understanding their roles in the opposing offense is crucial. With this information, you can devise a game plan that aims to exploit your opponent's vulnerabilities while neutralizing their strengths. This includes crafting defensive schemes, coverages, and blitz packages tailored to counter your specific opponent's offensive strategies.

In the process of developing a strong defensive game plan in flag football, it's important to delve deeper into each step and provide additional insights:

1. **Scout Your Opponents:**
   ✓ Film Study: Game film is a valuable resource for scouting opponents. Reviewing previous games can reveal patterns in their playcalling, formations, and player tendencies.
   ✓ Statistics: Analyze statistics from past games to identify trends. This can include passing yards, rushing yards, scoring distribution, and turnovers.
   ✓ Scouting Reports: If available, gather scouting reports or information from coaches who have faced the same opponents. Their insights can be invaluable.

2. **Understand Offensive Strategies:**
   ✓ Playbook Analysis: Try to get a sense of the opposing team's playbook. Are there recurring plays they favor in specific situations? Understanding their playbook can help you anticipate their actions.
   ✓ Field Position: Consider how field position influences your opponent's playcalling. Are they more aggressive in their approach when they have good field position, or do they tend to be conservative?

3. **Exploit Vulnerabilities:**
   ✓ Situational Weaknesses: Identify weaknesses that are situational. For example, do they struggle in short-yardage situations or have difficulty defending against deep passes?
   ✓ Red Zone Defense: Evaluate their performance in the red zone. Are they efficient at scoring touchdowns in these situations, or do they settle for field goals?

4. **Neutralize Strengths:**
   - ✓ Double Teaming: If your opponent has a standout receiver or playmaker, consider double-teaming or assigning extra coverage to limit their impact.
   - ✓ Quarterback Pressure: Apply consistent pressure on the quarterback to disrupt their timing. Sacks, hurries, and knockdowns can force turnovers or inaccurate throws.

5. **Defensive Schemes and Coverages:**
   - ✓ Variety: Incorporate a variety of defensive schemes and coverages to keep the offense guessing. Mixing zone and man coverage can make it challenging for the quarterback to read the defense.
   - ✓ Zone Blitzes: Implement zone blitz packages that involve unexpected blitzers dropping into coverage while maintaining pressure on the quarterback.

6. **Communication and Execution:**
   - ✓ Pre-Snap Communication: Encourage defenders to communicate pre-snap to adjust alignments and assignments based on the offensive formation.
   - ✓ Flag-Pulling Technique: Stress the importance of proper flag-pulling technique. Effective flag-pulling can quickly end a play and prevent yards after the catch.

7. **Adapt and Evolve:**
   - ✓ In-Game Observations: Assign a coach or player to focus on observing the opposing offense during the game. They can provide real-time feedback and suggest adjustments.

✓ Personnel Changes: Be willing to make personnel changes if certain defenders are struggling against specific matchups. Flexibility in player roles can be advantageous.

8. **Practice and Repetition:**

   ✓ Scrimmages: Arrange scrimmages or practice games against other teams to simulate game situations and test your defensive game plan.

   ✓ Game Situation Drills: Create drills that replicate common game situations, such as defending against a two-minute drill or sudden changes in field position.

Remember that developing a strong defensive game plan is an ongoing process. Continuously gather information on your opponents throughout the season and adjust your strategies accordingly. A well-prepared defense can be a significant asset in flag football, turning the tide of games and creating opportunities for success.

❖ Techniques for Flag-Pulling: Flag-pulling is the core of flag football defense. To excel in this aspect, players need to master various flag-pulling techniques. This involves understanding the correct hand placement and timing needed to dislodge the flag from the ball carrier's belt. Anticipation is key; defenders must read the ball carrier's movements and execute precise flag pulls to halt their progress. Additionally, we'll delve into strategies for intercepting passes, which can be a game-changer by not only halting the opponent's progress but also providing your offense with valuable possession.

Mastering Flag-Pulling Techniques in Flag Football:
Flag-pulling is the fundamental defensive skill in flag football, and excelling in this aspect is crucial for your team's success. Let's explore the key techniques and strategies for effective flag-pulling:

1. **Proper Hand Placement:**
   - ✓ Two-Hand Pull: The most common technique is the two- hand flag pull. Place one hand on each side of the ball carrier's flag, ensuring a secure grip. Pull the flag forcefully and swiftly to dislodge it.
   - ✓ One-Hand Pull: In situations where it's challenging to use both hands (e.g., when engaged with a blocker), you can execute a one-hand pull. Grip the flag with one hand and pull it while maintaining your balance.
2. **Timing and Anticipation:**
   - ✓ Read Ball Carrier's Movements: Anticipate the ball carrier's movements by reading their body language. Watch for cues like changes in direction, speed, or balance, which can signal when they're about to make a move.
   - ✓ React Swiftly: Once you anticipate the ball carrier's movement, react swiftly. Timing is critical. As soon as you see an opportunity, execute the flag pull with precision.

3. **Defensive Positioning:**
   - ✓ Maintain the Correct Angle: Position yourself at an angle to the ball carrier, not directly behind them. This angle provides a better perspective for flag pulling and reduces the risk of the ball carrier spinning away from you.
   - ✓ Stay Low and Balanced: Keep your body low and balanced to maintain stability. This posture allows you to make quick lateral movements and avoid being juked or sidestepped by the ball carrier.

4. **Defensive Strategies:**
   - ✓ Team Pursuit: Encourage your teammates to pursue the ball carrier as well. Multiple defenders converging on the ball carrier increase the chances of a successful flag pull.
   - ✓ Containment: In situations where you can't immediately pull the flag, focus on containment. Stay between the ball carrier and the end zone to prevent them from advancing further while waiting for an opportunity to make the flag pull.

5. **Intercepting Passes:**
   - ✓ Read the Quarterback: Intercepting passes requires excellent anticipation and reading the quarterback's eyes. Keep your eyes on the quarterback to gauge the intended target and the trajectory of the pass.
   - ✓ Positioning: Position yourself to intercept the pass by getting in the passing lane. This might involve moving

into the path of the ball or timing your jump to intercept it at its highest point.

✓ Hands and Timing: Use your hands to catch the ball, not your body. Extend your arms and reach for the pass at the right moment. Timing is crucial to ensure a clean interception.

✓ Secure the Ball: Once you intercept the pass, secure the ball and maintain possession. Be aware of potential tacklers and immediately transition to offense if possible.

Flag-pulling and intercepting passes are game-changing skills in flag football. By mastering these techniques and combining them with effective defensive positioning and teamwork, you can become a formidable defender who not only stops the opponent's progress but also creates opportunities for your team's offense.

8.2 Stopping the Run

Defending against running plays is a vital aspect of flag football defense. It requires a unique set of strategies and skills:

❖ Strategies for Defending Running Plays: Running plays are a staple of many flag football offenses. Defending against the run necessitates containment of ball carriers, maintaining gap integrity, and preventing significant gains. Pursuit angles are critical; defenders must take efficient angles to cut off running lanes and limit the ball carrier's options.

Proper leverage on the ball carrier and coordinated team-work to shut down running lanes are fundamental princi-ples in run defense.

Strategies for Defending Running Plays in Flag Football:
Defending running plays effectively in flag football requires a combination of sound fundamentals and teamwork. Here are key strategies to employ when facing running plays:

1. **Contain the Ball Carrier:**
   - ✓ Maintain Proper Angles: Defenders should take efficient angles to cut off running lanes and limit the ball carrier's options. Position yourself diagonally between the ball carrier and the sideline to force them toward the middle of the field, where pursuit from teammates can converge.
   - ✓ Stay Low and Balanced: Keep a low center of gravity and maintain balance to change direction quickly. This allows you to react to the ball carrier's movements and make effective tackles or flag pulls.

2. **Gap Integrity:**
   - ✓ Assign Gap Responsibilities: In flag football, as in tackle football, defenders should be responsible for specific gaps. Assign players to cover different areas of the field to prevent the ball carrier from finding gaps in the defense.
   - ✓ Seal Running Lanes: Ensure that defenders maintain discipline in their gap assignments. If one defender vacates their gap prematurely, it can create a running lane

for the ball carrier. Seal these running lanes by maintaining gap integrity.

3. **Proper Leverage:**

✓ Leverage on the Ball Carrier: Defenders should take the proper angle to leverage the ball carrier toward the sideline or back inside, depending on the defensive strategy. This makes it easier to pull the flag or make a tackle.

✓ Use Sideline as an Ally: The sideline can act as an additional defender. Encourage ball carriers to move toward the sideline, where it's easier for defenders to make flag pulls and stop their progress.

4. **Teamwork:**

✓ Coordinate Pursuit: Effective pursuit angles and coordinated teamwork are essential. Encourage defenders to communicate and work together to shut down running lanes. Multiple defenders converging on the ball carrier increase the chances of a successful flag pull or tackle.

✓ Swarm Tackles: When approaching the ball carrier, aim to swarm to the ball as a group. This approach can overwhelm the ball carrier and make it challenging for them to evade multiple defenders.

5. **Diagnose the Play:**

✓ Read the Play: Encourage defenders to read the play as it unfolds. Identifying the type of running play (e.g., sweep, dive, or pitch) can provide valuable clues on how to react and position yourself to make the flag pull or tackle.

6. **Maintain Discipline:**
   - ✓ Avoid Overcommitting: Defenders should avoid over-committing or getting caught out of position. Staying disciplined and maintaining gap responsibilities is crucial to containing running plays.

7. **Flag Pulling vs. Tackling:**
   - ✓ Flag Pulling Priority: In flag football, remember that flag pulling is the primary method of stopping the ball carrier. Prioritize flag pulls over physical tackles to prevent contact and promote safety.

By implementing these strategies and emphasizing teamwork and discipline, your defense can effectively shut down running plays in flag football. Maintaining proper angles, leveraging the sideline, and working together as a cohesive unit are key elements in containing the ball carrier and preventing significant gains on running plays.

- ❖ **Adjusting to Opponents' Offensive Schemes:** Every opponent brings a distinct set of offensive schemes and plays to the field. The ability to adapt your defensive strategy based on your opponent's style of play is a hallmark of a successful defense. This requires quick recognition of offensive formations, identifying tendencies, and making real-time adjustments during the game to counter your opponent's offensive strategies effectively. An adaptive defense can disrupt an opponent's rhythm and force them out of their comfort zone.

Adapting to Opponents' Offensive Schemes in Flag Football: Adapting your defensive strategy to counter your opponent's offensive schemes is a crucial aspect of a successful flag football defense. Here are key steps and considerations to help your defense adjust effectively:

1. **Pre-Game Preparation:**
    ✓ Scout Your Opponent: Prior to the game, conduct a scouting session to gain insights into your opponent's offensive tendencies. Pay attention to their favorite formations, plays, and key players.
    ✓ Identify Key Players: Recognize the opponents' key players, including the quarterback, top receivers, and ball carriers. Understanding their roles and tendencies will help you tailor your defensive approach.

2. **Recognize Offensive Formations:**
    ✓ Quick Recognition: Train your defenders to recognize offensive formations quickly. This includes identifying the number of receivers, their alignment, and potential motion or shifts before the snap.
    ✓ Formation-Based Adjustments: Have predefined defensive adjustments based on common offensive formations. For example, against a trip formation (three receivers to one side), you might shift defensive coverage to that side or employ zone coverage to limit passing options.

3. **In-Game Observations:**
    ✓ Stay Alert: During the game, maintain a high level of situational awareness. Watch for cues such as pre-snap

motion, the positioning of receivers, and the quarterback's body language.

✓ Communicate: Encourage constant communication among defenders. Use signals or verbal cues to relay adjustments and share observations with teammates.

4. **Real-Time Adjustments:**

✓ Be Adaptive: Be ready to adjust your defensive strategy in real time. If you notice recurring patterns or tendencies in the opponent's plays, adapt your coverage or alignment to counter their strategies.

✓ Mix-Up Coverages: Vary your defensive coverages to keep the offense guessing. Switch between man-to-man and zone coverage to disrupt the opponent's rhythm.

5. **Target Key Players:**

✓ Focus on Key Threats: Concentrate your defensive efforts on neutralizing the opponent's key players. For example, if the opponent has a dominant receiver, consider double coverage or assigning a "shadow" defender to cover them.

✓ Limit Options: Force the opponent to go to their secondary options by taking away their primary targets. Effective coverage of key players can disrupt the flow of their offense.

6. **Take Calculated Risks:**

✓ Blitz Packages: Implement well-timed blitz packages to apply pressure on the quarterback. However, be cautious about overcommitting, as this can leave your defense vulnerable to big plays.

✓ Interceptions: If you notice predictable passing routes, encourage defenders to take calculated risks and jump routes for potential interceptions.

7. **Post-Game Analysis:**
   ✓ Learn from Each Game: After each game, conduct a post- game analysis with your team. Discuss what worked, what didn't, and what adjustments could have been made. Use this feedback to improve your defense for future games.

Adapting to your opponent's offensive schemes requires a combination of preparation, awareness, and the ability to make quick decisions on the field. A flexible and adaptive defense can disrupt your opponent's rhythm, force them out of their comfort zone, and increase your chances of success in flag football.

A well-prepared defense can significantly impact the outcome of flag football games. By developing a strong defensive game plan, mastering flag-pulling techniques, and adapting to various offensive schemes, players can become stalwarts on the defensive side of the field, frustrating opponents and giving their team a competitive edge. In the upcoming chapters, we will explore advanced techniques, mental preparation, and the path to building a future in flag football, including college and scholarship opportunities.

CHAPTER 9
Advanced Techniques and Strategies

In Chapter 9, we will delve into the advanced aspects of flag football, including specialized roles and positions, trick plays, and advanced offensive schemes. These elements are essential for high- level competition and can give your team a significant edge on the field.

9.1   Specialized Roles and Positions

In high-level flag football, specialized positions and roles can give your team a strategic advantage. Let's delve deeper into these roles and explore advanced flag removal and coverage techniques:

❖ **Exploring Specialized Positions:** Specialized positions in flag football bring versatility and complexity to your team's strategy. One of the most critical specialized positions is the rusher. The rusher's primary role is to pressure the opposing quarterback, disrupt the timing of plays, and create opportunities for sacks and interceptions. To excel as a rusher, players must possess both speed and tactical awareness. It includes effectively mastering the art of timing rushes, choosing optimal angles to reach the quarterback, and employing various techniques to evade blockers. Understanding the nuances of the rusher position can significantly impact your team's defensive performance.

Expanding on the Role of the Rusher in Flag Football:
The rusher in flag football is a dynamic and influential position that can shape the game's outcome. Here, we'll delve deeper into the critical aspects of the rusher's role and strategies to excel in this specialized position:

1. **Disrupting Passing Plays:**
   - ✓ Timing and Strategy: Timing is crucial for a rusher. A well- timed rush can disrupt the quarterback's vision and rhythm, making it challenging to complete passes. Rushers must study the offense's snap count tendencies and adjust their timing accordingly.
   - ✓ Changing the Launch Point: Rushers can alter the quarterback's launch point by pressuring them to move within the pocket. Forcing the quarterback to throw on the run or from an uncomfortable position can lead to inaccurate passes and potential interceptions.

2. **Effective Flag-Pulling Techniques:**
   - ✓ Hand Placement: The rusher's primary goal is to pull the quarterback's flag before they release the pass. Flag pulling requires precise hand placement. Rushers should target the flag belt and practice accurate flag pulls to minimize the risk of grabbing clothing or missing the flag.
   - ✓ Two-Handed Approach: Using both hands to pull the flag simultaneously is often more effective than a one-handed grab. It reduces the chance of the quarterback evading the rush by spinning or sidestepping.

3. **Evading Blockers:**
    ✓ Blocker Recognition: Rushers must identify potential blockers and assess their intentions. Understanding how blockers are trying to impede your path can help devise strategies to evade or counter their efforts.
    ✓ Counter Moves: Rushers can employ counter moves such as rip, or swim moves to beat blockers. These techniques involve quick, fluid motions to get past blockers and reach the quarterback.

4. **Utilizing Speed and Agility:**
    ✓ Speed Off the Line: A rapid burst off the line of scrimmage is a rusher's best weapon. It can surprise the offensive line and make it challenging for them to react quickly.
    ✓ Change of Direction: Rushers should develop the ability to change direction rapidly. This agility helps when pursuing the quarterback as they move around the pocket.

5. **Team Communication:**
    ✓ Coordination with Defenders: Rushers should communicate with their fellow defenders, especially the players in the secondary. Effective coordination can improve coverage and increase the chances of disrupting passing plays.

6. **Versatility and Adaptability:**
    ✓ Counter Different Offenses: Being adaptable is critical. Rushers should be able to counter various offensive strategies. Some teams may employ a quick-release

passing game, while others rely on deeper routes. Rushers who can adjust their tactics accordingly become valuable assets.

7. **Psychological Pressure:**
    ✓ Mental Pressure: Rushers can also exert psychological pressure on the quarterback. Consistent rushes and near-sacks can make the quarterback feel hurried, leading to rushed decisions.

8. **Assessing Risk vs. Reward:**
    ✓ Balancing Aggression: Rushers must balance aggression with discipline. While it's essential to pressure the quarterback, overly aggressive rushes can leave openings for quick passes or runs. Rushers should assess the risk versus reward in each situation.

The rusher position in flag football combines physical attributes like speed and agility with mental acumen for timing and strategy. Excelling as a rusher requires continuous practice, studying opponents, and developing a versatile skill set. A skilled rusher can disrupt an opponent's offensive rhythm, create turnovers, and significantly impact the game's outcome.

❖ **Unveiling Advanced Flag Removal Techniques:** Flag removal is the linchpin of effective flag football defense. While basic flag-pulling is fundamental, advanced techniques take it to the next level. Advanced flag removal involves anticipating the ball carrier's movements, enhancing hand-eye coordination for swift flag pulls, and maintaining constant awareness of flag positions. These advanced techniques can become crucial in high-stakes games where the speed and precision of flag pulls can decide between victory and defeat.

Unveiling Advanced Flag Removal Techniques in Flag Football:

In flag football, advanced flag removal techniques can be the difference-maker in defense. While basic flag-pulling skills are essential, mastering advanced techniques can elevate your game to a higher level. These techniques require a combination of anticipation, hand-eye coordination, and heightened awareness of flag positions. Here, we delve into the intricacies of advanced flag removal techniques that can prove invaluable, especially in high- stakes games:

1. **Anticipating Ball Carrier's Movements:**
    ✓ Read and React: Advanced flag pullers become experts at reading the ball carrier's movements. They anticipate the ball carrier's direction and position themselves accordingly to maximize their chances of a successful flag pull.
    ✓ Study Opponent Tendencies: Observing the tendencies of specific opponents can provide valuable insights. Some ball carriers may have preferred moves or directions they tend to go when evading flag pulls. Recognizing these patterns can give you a significant advantage.

91

2. **Swift and Precise Flag Pulls:**
   - ✓ Hand Speed: Advanced flag pullers work on their hand speed. The quicker you can reach for the flag and make contact, the less time the ball carrier has to react and evade the pull.
   - ✓ Hand-Eye Coordination: Pinpoint accuracy is essential. Hand-eye coordination drills can help flag pullers target the flag and make precise grabs. Practicing catching moving objects or even juggling can enhance this skill.
   - ✓ Two-Handed Flag Pulls: When possible, advanced flag pullers often employ two-handed flag pulls. Using both hands simultaneously increases the chances of grabbing the flag cleanly.

3. **Awareness of Flag Positions:**
   - ✓ Constant Vigilance: Flag pullers maintain continuous awareness of the flag's position on the ball carrier's belt. It involves tracking the flag's movement and adjusting their approach as needed.
   - ✓ Flag Tucks and Hides: Some ball carriers attempt to hide their flags by tucking them or manipulating their clothing. Advanced flag pullers can detect these tactics and adjust their flag-pulling technique accordingly.

4. **Deceptive Techniques:**
   - ✓ Fakes and Feints: Just as offensive players use deception to elude defenders, flag pullers can employ fakes and feints to confuse the ball carrier. A sudden fake motion can cause the ball carrier to react, creating an opportunity for a successful flag pull.

✓ Angle Manipulation: Changing the approach angle when going for the flag can catch the ball carrier off guard. Slight adjustments in your positioning can make it more challenging for them to anticipate your flag pull.

5. **Practice and Repetition:**

✓ Drill Work: Consistent practice and drill work are crucial for mastering advanced flag removal techniques. Create scenarios that mimic game situations and practice flag pulls against teammates to refine your skills.

6. **Communication:**

✓ Team Coordination: In team defense, communication with fellow defenders is essential. Clear communication can help coordinate flag pulls, ensuring multiple defenders aren't attempting to pull the same flag simultaneously.

Advanced flag removal techniques require dedication, practice, and a deep understanding of your opponent's tendencies and the mechanics of flag pulling. These techniques can turn a good defender into an exceptional one, making you a valuable asset to your flag football team, especially in high-pressure situations where precision and speed are paramount.

❖ **Advanced Coverage Techniques: Effective** coverage skills are vital for limiting the opposing team's passing game. Advanced coverage techniques encompass various strategies, including man-to-man and zone coverage. In man-to-man coverage, defenders are responsible for shadowing specific receivers closely. Covering demands the ability to read the quarterback's eyes, anticipate the receiver's route, and maintain tight coverage throughout the play. Conversely, zone coverage involves defenders covering specific areas of the field instead of individual players. Understanding zone assignments, recognizing offensive patterns, and reacting quickly to the quarterback's throws are critical components of adequate zone coverage.

Exploring Advanced Coverage Techniques in Flag Football: Effective coverage skills are a cornerstone of successful flag football defense, particularly when facing strong passing offenses. Advanced coverage techniques encompass a range of strategies, including man-to-man and zone coverage. Here, we delve deeper into these advanced techniques:

Man-to-Man Coverage:
   Shadowing Specific Receivers:
✓ In man-to-man coverage, defenders closely shadow specific receivers throughout the play. Coverage This demands exceptional athleticism, agility, and anticipation.
✓ Reading the Quarterback's Eyes:
✓ Advanced man-to-man coverage involves sticking to your assigned receiver and reading the quarterback's eye; it can provide valuable insights into the intended target and the timing of the throw.
   Anticipating Receiver Routes:
✓ Effective man-to-man coverage requires anticipating the receiver's route based on initial movements and alignment.

94

This anticipation can help defenders position themselves advantageously.

Maintaining Tight Coverage:

✓ Staying close to the assigned receiver is crucial. Advanced defenders use their speed and agility to mirror the receiver's movements, making it challenging for the quarterback to complete passes.

Zone Coverage:

Understanding Zone Assignments:

✓ In zone coverage, defenders are responsible for specific field areas rather than individual players. Advanced defenders must deeply understand their zone assignments, recognizing where they need to be to provide optimal coverage.

Recognizing Offensive Patterns:

✓ Effective zone coverage involves recognizing offensive patterns and formations. This allows defenders to anticipate where potential threats will emerge within their zone and position themselves accordingly.

Reacting Quickly to Quarterback's Throws:

✓ Zone defenders must react swiftly to the quarterback's throws, closing the gap between themselves and the intended receiver. Advanced zone defenders have excellent reaction times and spatial awareness.

Additional Advanced Coverage Techniques:

Blending Man and Zone Concepts:

✓ Advanced defenders often blend man-to-man and zone concepts within a single play. This can involve covering a receiver man-to-man and transitioning into zone coverage as the play develops.

Baiting Quarterback Throws:

✓ Skilled defenders sometimes bait the quarterback into making a throw they intend to intercept. This involves subtly positioning themselves to make a play on the ball while still maintaining coverage on their assigned area or receiver.

Communication and Team Coordination:

✓ Effective communication among defenders is vital, particularly in zone coverage. Advanced defenders signal to each other, indicating when they're passing off receivers or alerting teammates to potential threats.

Film Study and Recognition:

✓ Advanced defenders study film to recognize offensive tendencies and quarterback behaviors. This preparation can lead to more informed decisions during the game.

Situational Awareness:

✓ Understanding the game situation is crucial. Advanced defenders adapt their coverage techniques based on down and distance, field position, and the score.

Mastery of advanced coverage techniques can significantly limit the opposing team's passing game, create turnovers, and ultimately influence the outcome of flag football games. These techniques require physical skills, football IQ, and situational awareness, all of which can be honed through dedicated practice and game experience.

9.2   Trick Plays and Advanced Schemes

Trick plays and advanced offensive schemes add an element of surprise and complexity to your playbook:

❖ **Mastering Advanced Offensive Schemes:** Advanced offensive schemes introduce sophistication and unpredictability to your team's strategies. These schemes can include option plays, misdirections, and screen plays. Option plays, for example, require precise timing and decision-making, as the quarterback has multiple choices, such as running or passing. Misdirection plays aim to confuse the defense by creating deceptive movements and patterns. Screen plays involve setting up blockers to create a screen for the ball carrier, allowing them to gain significant yardage. Mastering these advanced schemes can elevate your team's offensive capabilities and create opportunities for big plays.

Let's delve deeper into these advanced offensive schemes in flag football:

1.   **Option Plays:**

a. Read Option: In the read option, the quarterback reads the movement of a specific defender, often a defensive end or linebacker. If the defender commits to the quarterback, the QB hands the ball off to a running back; if the defender stays with the running back, the QB keeps the ball and runs. Timing and reading the defender's reactions are crucial.

b. Triple Option: This takes the read option a step further, with the quarterback having three options: keeping the ball, handing it off to a running back, or pitching it to another back or receiver. It requires precise execution and quick decision-making.

2.   Misdirection Plays:

a. Counter Plays: Counterplays involve deceptive movements and misdirection. The quarterback fakes a handoff in one direction while the running back carries the ball in the opposite direction. This can catch defenders off guard as they flow with the initial fake.

b. Reverse Plays: In reverse plays, the ball is handed off to a receiver who reverses the course and runs in the opposite direction. The goal is to create confusion and draw defenders out of position.

3.   Screen Plays:

a. Bubble Screen: In a bubble screen, a quick pass is thrown to a receiver positioned on the perimeter. Offensive linemen or other receivers set up blocks to create a "bubble" of space for the receiver to run. Timing between the quarterback and receiver is crucial.

b.   Swing Pass: The swing pass involves the quarterback quickly tossing the ball to a running back or receiver in the backfield. The receiver then has blockers in front to create a screen. It's effective in short-yardage situations.

4.   Trick Plays:

a.   Double Pass: This trick play involves two forward passes in a single play. The first pass is typically a lateral to a receiver or running back, who throws a forward pass to another receiver. It requires precise timing and the element of surprise.

b.   Flea Flicker: In a flea flicker, the quarterback hands off the ball to a running back, then tosses it back to the quarterback. The quarterback can then throw a deep pass to a receiver who has gotten behind the defense.

5.   Spread Offense:

a.   Four-Wide Formation: A common formation in the spread offense is having four receivers spread out wide. This stretches the defense horizontally, creating one-on-one matchups and openings in the middle of the field.

b.   Quick Passes: The spread offense often employs quick, short passes to exploit the space created by the wide receiver alignment. Receivers use their agility to gain yards after the catch.

6.   No-Huddle Offense:

a.   Tempo Control: The no-huddle offense keeps the tempo fast, not allowing the defense time to substitute or rest. This can lead to defensive confusion and mismatches.

b.   Silent Snap Counts: To maintain the element of surprise, the no- huddle offense may use silent snap counts, with the offensive linemen watching the quarterback's signals for when to snap the ball.

7.   Shotgun Formation:

a.   Pass-First Formation: The shotgun formation is often used when the offense intends to pass the ball. It gives the quarterback a better view of the field and additional decision-making time.

b.   Quick Releases: Quarterbacks in the shotgun can release the ball quickly, which is advantageous for short and intermediate passing plays.

8.   Audibles and Checkdowns:

a.   Pre-Snap Adjustments: The quarterback can change the play or adjust routes based on what they see from the defense before the snap. This adaptability can exploit defensive weaknesses.

b.   Checkdowns: If the primary receiving options are covered, the quarterback can "check down" by passing to a running back or receiver in a short, safe zone to gain positive yardage.

Mastering these advanced offensive schemes requires a combination of football IQ, timing, and execution. Teams that incorporate these schemes effectively into their playbook can keep the defense on its toes, create mismatches, and generate big plays, ultimately leading to success in flag football games and tournaments.

❖ Trick Plays for Outsmarting Opponents: Trick plays are a thrilling aspect of flag football that relies on deception and surprise to confound opponents. Plays like the flea flicker, where the ball is lateraled back to the quarterback after a handoff, or the hook and ladder, where a receiver laterals to a teammate after a catch, can lead to explosive gains or touchdowns when executed correctly. Double passes, where a receiver becomes a passer, add unpredictability to your offense. These trick plays require meticulous timing, precision, and teamwork to succeed.

Let's explore these trick plays in more detail and understand how they can be executed effectively in flag football:

1. **Flea Flicker:**
   ✓ Execution: The play starts with the quarterback handing the ball off to a running back, who then begins to run forward as if they intend to carry out a rushing play. Just before reaching the line of scrimmage, the running back laterals (tosses) the ball back to the quarterback, who is now behind the line of scrimmage. The quarterback then has the option to throw a pass downfield to a receiver.
   ✓ Key Elements: Timing is crucial in the flea flicker. The running back must lateral the ball at the right moment, and the quarterback needs to have a receiver breaking free downfield. Receivers should act as if they're running a regular route initially to draw defenders in before breaking deep.

2. **Hook and Ladder:**
   - ✓ Execution: This play involves a receiver catching a short pass and immediately lateraling (pitching) the ball to a trailing teammate who is typically running a deeper route. The lateral creates a surprise element that can catch the defense off guard and lead to significant yardage or a touchdown.
   - ✓ Key Elements: Timing and communication between the initial receiver and the player receiving the lateral are critical. The lateral must be executed quickly and accurately. Receivers must be aware of their surroundings to make the lateral under pressure.

3. **Double Pass:**
   - ✓ Execution: In a double pass, a receiver becomes a passer. The quarterback starts with a short pass to a receiver positioned to throw a second pass downfield. The second pass can target another receiver or even the original quarterback if they've moved into a receiving position.
   - ✓ Key Elements: This play relies on deception, as the defense may initially need to recognize that the receiver intends to pass the ball again. The receiver must have a strong arm and accuracy to make an effective second pass.

4. **Statue of Liberty:**
   - ✓ Execution: This trick play involves the quarterback faking a pass but keeping the ball hidden behind their back. Meanwhile, a running back positions themselves behind

the quarterback, appearing as if they're about to receive a handoff. The quarterback then reveals the hidden ball and either carries out a run or throws a pass.

- ✓ Key Elements: Timing and coordination are crucial. The defense should be tricked into thinking a pass is coming, only to be surprised by the actual play. The running back's positioning and movements are key to selling the fake.

5. **Fake Punt or Field Goal:**
   - ✓ Execution: In a fake punt or field goal attempt, the special teams unit initially lines up as if they're going to kick the ball. However, the player with the ball can run or pass instead of kicking. This play often converts a fourth down or catches the defense off guard.
   - ✓ Key Elements: Timing and execution are critical. The punter or kicker must be prepared to make a quick decision based on the defensive alignment and whether there's an opportunity to convert the play.

These trick plays can be game-changers when executed effectively. However, they also come with a degree of risk, as any miscommunication or mishandling of the ball can lead to turnovers. Teams should practice these plays extensively to ensure that all players understand their roles and timing, making them a valuable addition to the playbook for those critical moments when deception can turn the tide of a game.

By incorporating specialized roles and positions, mastering advanced flag removal and coverage techniques, and adding trick plays and advanced offensive schemes to your playbook, you can raise your flag football game to an elite level. These advanced strategies and techniques will make you an invaluable asset to your team and enhance your enjoyment and success in high-level flag football competitions. In the upcoming chapters, we will explore further aspects of building a future in flag football, including opportunities for college play and scholarship possibilities.

CHAPTER 10
Building a Future in Flag Football

10.1 College and Scholarship Opportunities

Flag football opens doors to exciting opportunities for individuals looking to continue their involvement in the sport while pursuing higher education:

❖ **Discovering Pathways to College:** Many colleges and universities nationwide offer flag football programs, ranging from club sports to intramurals. Some colleges even have varsity flag football teams. Joining a flag football program at the collegiate level can be a fantastic way to continue playing while pursuing your academic goals. We will explore strategies for identifying colleges that offer flag football as an extracurricular activity and discuss the advantages of being part of such teams.

Expanding on the topic of discovering pathways to college flag football, let's delve deeper into some strategies for researching and identifying colleges that offer opportunities for flag football players:

❖ **Online Research:** The internet is valuable for researching colleges and their sports programs. Start by visiting the official websites of colleges and universities you're interested in. Look for sections related to athletics, intramural sports, or club sports. Many colleges provide information about their flag football programs, including team schedules, try-out details, and contact information for coaches or program coordinators.

❖ College Athletics Directories: Several online directories and databases specialize in college athletics. Websites like the NCAA (National Collegiate Athletic Association) and NAIA (National Association of Intercollegiate Athletics) provide information about colleges with varsity sports programs, including flag football. You can search for colleges by location, division, or sport.

❖ Contact Admissions or Student Affairs: Contact the admissions or student affairs offices of colleges you're interested in and inquire about flag football programs. They can provide information about club sports, intramurals, and any other flag football opportunities available on campus.

❖ Connect with Current Players: If you know someone who attends a college with a flag football program, consider contacting them for insights. Current players can provide valuable information about the team's culture, level of competition, and how to get involved.

❖ Attend College Fairs and Showcases: College fairs and showcases often feature representatives from various colleges and universities. These events can be an excellent opportunity to speak directly with college sports program representatives and learn about flag football opportunities.

❖ Visit College Campuses: Visit the campuses of colleges you're considering. While there, you can inquire about flag football programs, meet with coaches or program administrators, and get a feel for the overall sports culture at the college.

❖ Advantages of Being Part of a College Flag Football Program:

❖ Skill Development: College-level play typically offers a higher level of competition, allowing you to improve your skills and knowledge of the game.

❖ Networking: Being part of a college team introduces you to a network of fellow athletes, coaches, and alums who can provide support and opportunities in the future.

❖ Discipline and Time Management: Balancing academics and athletics in college teaches valuable time management and discipline, transferable skills to other areas of life.

❖ Leadership Opportunities: College flag football programs often offer leadership roles, such as team captain or club officer, which can enhance your leadership abilities.

❖ Physical Fitness: Participation in college sports keeps you physically active and promotes a healthy lifestyle.

❖ Personal Growth: Playing at the college level can foster personal growth by pushing you to overcome challenges, set goals, and develop perseverance.

❖ In conclusion, discovering and joining a college flag football program can be an enriching experience that combines your passion for the sport with your pursuit of higher education. By researching colleges, reaching out to program representatives, and understanding the advantages of college-level play, you can make an informed decision about your athletic and academic journey.

❖ Scholarship Opportunities: While flag football scholarships may not be as widespread as those for traditional sports, they are available for talented players. We will delve into how to find and apply for flag football scholarships, emphasizing the importance of creating an impressive player profile, showcasing your skills through highlight videos, and participating in showcase events to attract the attention of college recruiters. Earning a scholarship can support your education and allow you to continue your passion for flag football at the collegiate level.

Expanding on the topic of scholarship opportunities in flag football, let's explore some key strategies and considerations for finding and applying for these scholarships:

Create an Impressive Player Profile:
✓ Resume: Develop a comprehensive player resume that includes your flag football experience, achievements, honors, and statistics. Highlight any leadership roles, such as team captain, and your contributions to the team's success.
✓ Academic Record: Maintain a solid academic record. Many scholarships, including those for flag football, consider your academic performance.
✓ Character References: Obtain character references from coaches, teachers, or community leaders who can vouch for

your sportsmanship, dedication, and character both on and off the field.

Prepare Highlight Videos:

✓ Create Highlight Reels: Compile highlight videos showcasing your skills, game performance, and notable plays. Use video editing software to create professional-looking reels that capture your best moments.

✓ Game Footage: Include clips from actual games that demonstrate your abilities in flag football, such as passing, receiving, flag-pulling, and defensive plays.

✓ Online Presence: Upload your highlight videos to platforms like YouTube or Vimeo and share the links in your scholarship applications. Make sure your videos are easily accessible to college recruiters.

Participate in Showcase Events:

✓ Identify Showcase Opportunities: Research and attend flag football showcase events or tournaments where college recruiters may be present. These events provide a platform to showcase your skills and interact with recruiters.

✓ Perform Consistently: Make the most of showcase events by demonstrating your abilities and teamwork. College recruiters often attend these events to scout potential scholarship recipients.

Research Scholarship Opportunities:

✓ Identify Organizations: Research organizations, foundations, and associations that offer flag football scholarships.

These may include local sports clubs, flag football leagues, or national flag football organizations.

- ✓ College Programs: Explore colleges and universities with varsity or club flag football teams. Some of these institutions may offer scholarships to talented players.
- ✓ Contact College Coaches:
- ✓ Reach Out: Contact the coaches of flag football programs you are interested in, express your interest in their program, and inquire about scholarship opportunities.
- ✓ Share Your Profile: Provide coaches with your player resume, highlight videos, and other relevant information showcasing your skills and commitment to the sport.

Apply Strategically:

- ✓ Scholarship Applications: Prepare and submit scholarship applications on time. Follow the instructions carefully, and tailor your applications to each scholarship opportunity.
- ✓ Scholar-Athlete Balance: Emphasize your dedication to flag football, academics, and community involvement. Many scholarships value well-rounded scholar-athletes.
- ✓ Stay Persistent:
- ✓ Scholarship Hunt: Understand that the scholarship application process can be competitive and may require persistence. Apply for multiple scholarships to maximize your chances of success.
- ✓ Follow-up: Be encouraged if you receive an immediate response. Follow up with coaches and scholarship committees to express your continued interest.

A flag football scholarship can be a significant achievement supporting your educational and athletic aspirations. By proactively building your player profile, showcasing your skills through videos and events, and actively seeking scholarship opportunities, you can increase your chances of securing financial aid to pursue your academic and flag football goals.

10.2 Coaching and Officiating

Flag football provides avenues for staying connected with the sport and giving back:

❖ **Exploring Coaching Roles:** Coaching offers a rewarding way to contribute to the sport's growth and development. Whether you have playing experience or a deep passion for flag football, becoming a coach allows you to mentor young athletes, share your knowledge, and instill a love for the sport in others. We will explore the qualifications and steps required to become a certified flag football coach, including coaching courses and certifications. Effective coaching strategies, leadership skills, and communication techniques will also be discussed to help you become a successful coach.

Expanding on the topic of exploring coaching roles in flag football, let's dive into the qualifications, steps, and essential skills needed to become a certified and effective flag football coach: Qualifications and Steps to Become a Certified Flag Football Coach:

❖ Playing Experience: While not always mandatory, having prior flag football playing experience can be a valuable asset for a coach. It provides firsthand knowledge of the game's dynamics and strategies.

Coaching Courses and Certifications:
✓ Flag Football Coaching Courses: Many organizations and governing bodies offer coaching courses specific to flag football. These courses cover various aspects of coaching, including game strategies, player development, and safety protocols.

✓ Certification Programs: Enroll in flag football coaching certification programs. These programs often include both classroom learning and practical coaching experience. Completion of these programs may be required for coaching at certain levels or organizations.

✓ Background Checks: Depending on the organization or league you wish to coach in, you may be required to undergo background checks and clearances to ensure the safety of young athletes.

✓ Attend Coaching Clinics: Participate in coaching clinics and workshops led by experienced coaches and experts in flag football. These events provide valuable insights, networking opportunities, and hands-on coaching experience.

✓ Join Coaching Associations: Consider becoming a member of coaching associations or organizations dedicated to flag football. These associations often provide resources, mentorship, and opportunities for continuing education.

✓ Essential Skills and Strategies for Effective Coaching:

Leadership Skills:

✓ Positive Role Model: Lead by example and demonstrate sportsmanship, integrity, and respect for players, officials, and opponents.

✓ Effective Communication: Develop strong communication skills to convey instructions, provide feedback, and build rapport with your team.

Player Development:

✓ Individual Skills: Focus on improving the unique skills of each player, including passing, receiving, flag-pulling, and defensive techniques.

✓ Teamwork: Emphasize teamwork, cooperation, and synergy among players to enhance overall performance.

Game Strategies:

✓ Offensive and Defensive Schemes: Develop and implement effective offensive and defensive strategies tailored to your team's strengths and opponent analysis.

✓ In-Game Adjustments: Be prepared to make real- time adjustments during games based on the opponent's tactics and game situations.

Safety and Injury Prevention:

✓ Safety Education: Educate players on safety measures, including proper warm-up, hydration, and injury prevention techniques.

✓ First Aid Awareness: Familiarize yourself with basic first aid practices and be prepared to respond to minor injuries on the field.

Motivation and Mentorship:

✓ Motivate Players: Inspire and motivate players to give their best effort, set goals, and persevere through challenges.

✓ Mentorship: Offer guidance and mentorship to help players excel in the sport and develop life skills and character.

Organization and Planning:

✓ Practice Plans: Create well-structured practice plans that include drills, exercises, and scrimmage sessions to maximize player development.

✓ Game Preparation: Develop pre-game and post-game routines and strategies to ensure your team is well- prepared for each match.

Continuous Learning:

✓ Stay Informed: Keep up with the latest developments in flag football, coaching techniques, and rule changes by attending coaching clinics and seminars.

✓ Feedback and Evaluation: Provide constructive feedback to players and conduct regular assessments to track their progress.

Becoming a certified flag football coach and effectively guiding young athletes requires a combination of knowledge, experience, and a commitment to player development and safety. By pursuing coaching courses and certifications, developing essential coaching skills, and staying dedicated to continuous learning, you can contribute significantly to the growth and success of flag football in your community.

❖ **Officiating Opportunities:** Officiating is a crucial aspect of flag football, ensuring that games are played fairly and according to the rules. If you are interested in officiating, we will discuss becoming a certified flag football official, which typically involves training and certification programs. Being a flag football official requires a thorough understanding of the rules, excellent judgment, and impartiality to maintain the integrity of the game.

Expanding on the topic of exploring officiating opportunities in flag football, let's delve into the process of becoming a certified flag football official and the key responsibilities and skills required for this critical role:

Becoming a Certified Flag Football Official:
Training and Education:
✓ Flag Football Officiating Courses: Enroll in flag football officiating courses by recognized organizations or governing bodies. These courses cover the rules, mechanics, and best practices for officiating flag football games.
✓ Certification Programs: Many flag football leagues and associations require officials to complete certification programs. These programs often include written exams, on-field training, and evaluations.
Rulebook Familiarity:
✓ In-Depth Knowledge: Acquire a comprehensive understanding of the flag football rulebook, including rules related to gameplay, penalties, and player conduct.

✓ Updates and Changes: Stay informed about any rule changes or updates issued by the governing body, as rules may evolve.

On-Field Training:

✓ Practical Experience: Gain hands-on experience by officiating flag football games at various levels, including youth, amateur, and competitive leagues.

✓ Mentorship: Seek mentorship from experienced officials who can provide guidance and feedback to help you improve your officiating skills.

Equipment and Uniform:

✓ Officiating Gear: Acquire the necessary officiating equipment, including a whistle, flag belt, penalty flag, and a down indicator.

✓ Official Uniform: Dress in the official uniform designated by the league or organization you officiate for. This typically includes a striped shirt, black pants, and appropriate footwear.

Key Responsibilities and Skills of a Flag Football Official:
Rule Enforcement:

✓ Fair Play: Ensure both teams adhere to the game's rules, promoting fair play and sportsmanship.

✓ Penalty Calls: Accurately identify and signal penalties, enforce penalty yardage, and communicate infractions to coaches and players.

Game Management:

✓ Game Timing: Manage the game clock, including starting and stopping it as necessary, to ensure the timely progress of the game.

✓ Ball Placement: Determine the correct spot for ball placement, including first downs and touchdowns.

Communication:

✓ Clear Communication: Use clear and concise signals and verbal communication to convey decisions and rulings to players, coaches, and spectators.

✓ Conflict Resolution: Handle disputes and conflicts on the field professionally and impartially, working to de-escalate tensions.

Positioning and Mechanics:

✓ Proper Positioning: Maintain the correct positioning on the field to have a clear view of the action and make accurate calls.

✓ Mechanics: Follow established mechanics for flag football officiating, including positioning for different plays and situations.

Judgment and Consistency:

✓ Game Flow: Make judgment calls to keep the game flowing smoothly while maintaining consistency in decision-making throughout the game.

✓ Player Safety: Prioritize player safety and immediately act in potentially dangerous situations.

Knowledge and Continuous Learning:

✓ Rulebook Updates: Stay up-to-date with any changes or updates to the flag football rulebook.

✓ Rules Interpretation: Be prepared to accurately interpret and apply rules in real-time situations.

✓ Impartiality:

✓ Neutral Officiating: Maintain impartiality and avoid favoritism or bias toward any team or player.

Flag football officiating ensures the game's integrity and participants' safety. Pursuing training and certification, developing solid officiating skills, and upholding fairness and professionalism on the field. You can contribute to the success of flag football in your community and provide a valuable service to the sport.

10.3 Promoting Flag Football

Flag football has the potential to thrive and become a prominent sport in your community:

❖ **Promoting Flag Football:** You can play a pivotal role in promoting flag football in your community. We will explore strategies for engaging with local schools, organizing flag football leagues or tournaments, and creating a positive and inclusive flag football culture. Encouraging youth participation, emphasizing teamwork and sportsmanship, and fostering a sense of community around the sport can contribute to its growth and popularity.

Let's delve deeper into these strategies for promoting flag football in your community:

1. **Engaging with Local Schools:**
   - ✓ School Programs: Work closely with school administrators and physical education teachers to integrate flag football into the school's sports curriculum. This could involve offering flag football as an option during physical education classes or organizing intramural flag football leagues within the school.
   - ✓ Youth Outreach: Conduct workshops and introductory sessions for students to learn about flag football. Host "Flag Football Days" at schools, where students can participate in fun flag football activities to get a taste of the sport.

2. **Organizing Flag Football Leagues and Tournaments:**
   - ✓ Youth Leagues: Establishing youth flag football leagues provides a structured and competitive outlet for young athletes. Leagues can be organized based on age groups, allowing children to play with their peers.
   - ✓ Community Tournaments: Hosting flag football tournaments open to participants of all ages can generate excitement and interest in the sport. Consider themed tournaments, charity events, or special tournaments to attract different demographics.

3. **Coaching and Officiating Development:**
   - ✓ Coach Training: Offer coaching clinics and certification programs that teach the fundamentals of coaching and emphasize positive coaching techniques, sportsmanship, and safety protocols.
   - ✓ Officiating Clinics: Ensure that your community has well- trained referees and officials. Organize officiating clinics to recruit and train individuals interested in overseeing flag football games.

4. **Youth Engagement and Mentorship:**
   - ✓ Youth Camps: Organize flag football camps during school breaks or summer vacations. These camps can focus on skill development, teamwork, and character building. Experienced coaches can lead these camps and provide mentorship.
   - ✓ Mentorship Programs: Create mentorship programs where seasoned flag football players, coaches, or community leaders act as mentors to younger or less experienced participants. This helps in skill development and builds a sense of community.

5. **Inclusivity and Diversity:**
   - ✓ Girls and Women's Participation: Promote gender equality in flag football by encouraging girls and women to participate. Establish girls-only or women's flag football leagues and teams.
   - ✓ Inclusive Policies: Implement and promote policies emphasizing inclusivity and non-discrimination based on

age, gender, skill level, or physical ability. Ensure that all participants feel welcome and valued.

6. **Community Outreach:**
   ✓ Local Events: Participate in community events and fairs to showcase flag football. Set up informational booths, demonstrations, or mini-games to engage with the community and attract new participants.
   ✓ School Partnerships: Collaborate with local schools, community centers, and youth organizations to introduce flag football to a broader audience. Offer workshops or introductory sessions at these locations.

7. **Social Media and Online Presence:**
   ✓ Online Promotion: Maintain an active online presence through social media platforms, dedicated websites, or forums. Share regular updates, schedules, and success stories, and highlight the positive impact of flag football in your community.
   ✓ Interactive Platforms: Create online platforms where community members can discuss flag football-related topics, share their experiences, and connect with others interested in the sport.

8. **Volunteer Support:**
   ✓ Recruit Volunteers: Encourage community members, especially those with flag football experience, to volunteer as coaches, officials, organizers, or mentors. Recognize and appreciate their contributions to the sport.

✓ Volunteer Training: Provide training and resources for volunteers to ensure they are equipped with the necessary skills and knowledge to contribute effectively.

9. **Facilities and Equipment:**

✓ Accessible Fields: Advocate for accessible and well-maintained playing fields and facilities where flag football can be played safely. Collaborate with local authorities and organizations to improve or create new facilities.

✓ Equipment Access: Ensure that flag football equipment, such as flags, footballs, and protective gear, is readily available to participants and teams. Consider fundraising or sponsorship opportunities to provide equipment to underserved communities.

10. **Celebrate Flag Football Culture:**

✓ Flag Football Day: Designate a specific day as "Flag Football Day" in your community. Organize special events, exhibitions, or tournaments on this day to celebrate the sport and its positive impact on the community.

✓ Community Awards: Recognize outstanding contributions to flag football in your community through awards or accolades. Celebrate the achievements of players, coaches, officials, and volunteers.

By implementing these strategies and fostering a positive, inclusive, and enthusiastic flag football culture in your community, you can help ensure that flag football becomes a vibrant and integral part of your local sports landscape, inspiring youth and adults alike to embrace the sport and its values.

❖ **Shaping the Sport's Future:** Your dedication and passion can help shape the future of flag football. We will discuss how to connect with flag football organizations, participate in advocacy efforts, and contribute to the development of the sport at the local, regional, and national levels. Whether through volunteering, organizing events, or advocating for increased recognition of flag football, your involvement can have a lasting impact on the sport's trajectory.

Shaping the future of flag football requires proactive engagement and advocacy. Here are ways to get involved and contribute to the sport's growth:

1. **Connect with Flag Football Organizations:**
   ✓ National and Regional Bodies: Join national and regional flag football organizations. These organizations often have resources, contacts, and initiatives to promote and develop the sport.
   ✓ Local Leagues and Clubs: Become a part of local flag football leagues, clubs, or teams. Engage with the community and network with fellow enthusiasts.

2. **Volunteer and Coach:**
   ✓ Youth Coaching: Volunteer as a youth flag football coach or mentor. Your guidance can positively influence young players and help them develop both athletically and personally.

123

- ✓ Organizational Roles: Consider taking up leadership roles within flag football organizations or clubs. These positions may involve event planning, fundraising, or administrative responsibilities.

3. **Advocate for Recognition:**
   - ✓ School Programs: Advocate for the inclusion of flag football in school sports programs. Engage with school boards, administrators, and parent-teacher associations to emphasize the sport's benefits and safety.
   - ✓ Community Support: Build support within your community by organizing meetings, workshops, or presentations that educate community members, leaders, and decision-makers about the advantages of flag football.

4. **Hosting Flag Football Events:**
   - ✓ Tournaments and Clinics: Organize flag football tournaments, clinics, and workshops to promote the sport. These events can attract new players and generate interest in your region.
   - ✓ Charity Events: Consider hosting charity flag football events that showcase the sport and contribute to community causes. This can help build a positive image for the sport and its participants.

5. **Collaborate with Schools:**
   - ✓ School Partnerships: Collaborate with local schools to introduce flag football programs. Offer assistance in starting and maintaining school flag football teams and leagues.

✓ Youth Outreach: Initiate outreach programs that involve visiting schools and conducting flag football demonstrations or mini-games to engage students and spark their interest.

6. **Educational Initiatives:**

✓ Flag Football Clinics: Organize educational clinics on flag football rules, strategies, and safety for players, coaches, and parents. These clinics can enhance the overall understanding and appreciation of the sport.

✓ Youth Empowerment: Promote flag football as a means of youth empowerment, character development, and teamwork. Showcase stories of young athletes who have benefited from their involvement in the sport.

7. **Collaborate with Other Sports:**

✓ Multi-Sport Events: Partner with other sports organizations to host multi-sport events or festivals. This can introduce flag football to individuals who may not have considered it otherwise.

✓ Youth Sports Initiatives: Advocate for flag football's inclusion in broader youth sports initiatives that promote physical activity and healthy lifestyles.

8. **Online and Social Media Presence:**

✓ Online Advocacy: Use social media and platforms to advocate for flag football. Share success stories, news, and relevant content to create a digital community of flag football enthusiasts.

✓ Engage with Decision-Makers: Reach out to elected officials, sports governing bodies, and sports commissioners to highlight the importance of flag football and its positive impact on the community.

9. **Data and Research:**

✓ Flag Football Research: Encourage and support research on the benefits and impact of flag football on youth development, physical fitness, and community cohesion. Data-driven insights can bolster advocacy efforts.

10. **Support Inclusivity:**

✓ Promote Diversity: Emphasize the inclusive nature of flag football and actively promote participation among individuals of diverse backgrounds, genders, and abilities.

Remember that your commitment and efforts can positively change your local and regional flag football communities. By connecting with organizations, advocating for recognition, and actively participating in the sport's development, you can help shape a brighter future for flag football. Your passion and dedication will inspire others to join and contribute to the sport's growth.

By exploring college and scholarship opportunities, considering coaching and officiating roles, and actively promoting flag football in your community, you can build a future in flag football that not only benefits your personal development but also contributes to the sport's growth and success. Flag football offers a vibrant and inclusive community, and your commitment can make a meaningful difference in the lives of aspiring athletes and the sport's overall development. This chapter equips you with the knowledge and tools to pursue your flag football aspirations beyond the playing field.

CHAPTER 11
Beyond the Field: Flag Football Culture

Chapter 11 will explore the vibrant flag football culture beyond the playing field. This chapter will focus on connecting with the flag football community, finding opportunities for competitive play and tournaments, and understanding the broader role of flag football in personal development.

11.1   Connecting with the Flag Football Community

Flag football is not just a sport; it's a thriving community where players of all ages and backgrounds come together to share their passion for the game. Here's how you can connect with this dynamic community:

❖ **Joining Flag Football Communities and Organizations:** Flag football communities and organizations exist at various levels, from local clubs to national associations. These groups provide a platform for players to connect, share experiences, and stay informed about the latest developments in the sport. Engaging with these communities through social media, online forums, or local clubs can help you build lasting relationships, access valuable resources, and stay updated on flag football news, events, and opportunities.

Expanding your involvement in flag football communities and organizations can be a rewarding and impactful journey. Here are some additional strategies and insights to help you connect more deeply with the flag football world:

1. **Attend Flag Football Workshops and Clinics:**
    - ✓ Look for flag football workshops, coaching clinics, or player development sessions in your area. These events often feature experienced coaches and players who can provide valuable insights and hands-on training.

2. **Start Your Flag Football Initiative:**
    - ✓ If there are no flag football programs or clubs in your area, consider starting your own. Gather interested players, find a suitable field or facility, and organize games or practices. Building a local community can attract more players and generate interest in the sport.

3. **Volunteer for Youth Programs:**
    - ✓ Many flag football organizations run youth development programs. Volunteering as a coach or mentor for young players can be immensely rewarding. It also helps to nurture the next generation of flag football enthusiasts.

4. **Engage in Social Media Groups:**
    - ✓ Participate actively in flag football-related social media groups, where enthusiasts share tips, videos, and experiences. These platforms are excellent for networking and staying updated on sports trends.

5. **Collaborate with Local Schools:**
    - ✓ Reach out to schools in your area to discuss introducing flag football as an extracurricular activity or as part of

physical education programs. Partnering with educational institutions can be a powerful way to expand the sport's reach.

6. **Organize Flag Football Tournaments:**
   - ✓ Host your flag football tournaments or leagues, inviting teams from nearby regions to participate. Organizing events can build community and attract more players to the sport.

7. **Advocate for Inclusivity:**
   - ✓ Promote inclusivity within the flag football community by encouraging participation from all genders, age groups, and skill levels. Advocate for fair play, sportsmanship, and a welcoming environment for everyone.

8. **Share Your Story:**
   - ✓ Share your flag football journey and experiences through blogs, social media, or local news outlets. Your story can inspire others to get involved in the sport.

9. **Join Flag Football Associations:**
   - ✓ Investigate if there are regional or national flag football associations that you can join. These associations often provide resources, networking opportunities, and a platform to voice your ideas and concerns.

10. **Mentorship and Coaching:**
    - ✓ Consider offering your expertise as a mentor or coach to aspiring players. Providing guidance and support can significantly impact their development and love for the sport.

11. **Supportive Fanship:**
   ✓ Even if you're not actively playing or coaching, being a dedicated fan and attending games or events can contribute to the sport's vibrant atmosphere. Cheer for your local teams and promote a positive fan culture.

12. **Explore Officiating Roles:**
   ✓ If you're interested in officiating, consider taking courses and certifications to become a qualified flag football official. This can be a rewarding way to contribute to the game's integrity.
   ✓ Remember that your passion for flag football and willingness to get involved can make a real difference in your local and regional flag football community. Whether you're an athlete, coach, volunteer, or advocate, your commitment helps foster a thriving flag football culture for all to enjoy.
   ✓ Finding Opportunities for Competitive Play and Tournaments: Flag football offers various playing opportunities, from recreational leagues to highly competitive tournaments. These events bring players together for the thrill of competition and camaraderie. Participating in local, regional, or national flag football tournaments can be an exciting way to challenge your skills and showcase your talent. We'll explore how to identify and register for these competitions, highlighting the benefits of competitive play in your flag football journey.

11.2 Personal Development Through Flag Football

Flag football goes beyond physical prowess; it fosters personal growth and development:

❖ Understanding the Broader Role of Flag Football in Personal Growth: Flag football imparts valuable life skills that extend far beyond the field's boundaries. These skills include teamwork, leadership, discipline, resilience, and the ability to handle pressure. We will delve into how these qualities acquired through flag football can positively influence other areas of your life. Whether it's excelling in academics, advancing in your career, or nurturing meaningful personal relationships, the lessons learned on the flag football field can be applied to various life situations.

Let's delve deeper into how the life skills developed in flag football can positively influence various aspects of personal growth:

1. **Teamwork and Collaboration:**
   ✓ Workplace Dynamics: The ability to collaborate effectively learned in flag football can be applied to workplace dynamics. Working well within a team, being receptive to others' ideas, and contributing to group goals are essential in professional settings.
   ✓ Community Engagement: Teamwork skills can also be valuable in community engagement and volunteer

work. Being part of a collective effort to address social issues or support a cause requires collaboration.

2. **Leadership Development:**
   - ✓ Career Advancement: Leadership skills honed in flag football can propel individuals into leadership positions. The capacity to guide, motivate, and inspire others can lead to promotions and career growth.
   - ✓ Mentoring: Experienced flag football players can become mentors to younger athletes, passing on their knowledge and leadership skills. This mentorship can extend to other areas, such as tutoring or coaching.

3. **Discipline and Commitment:**
   - ✓ Academic Achievement: The discipline developed in flag football can contribute to academic success. Students who are dedicated to their studies and manage their time effectively often perform better in school.
   - ✓ Career Excellence: In the professional realm, disciplined individuals tend to be more organized, meet deadlines, and exhibit consistent work ethics, which employers highly value.

4. **Resilience and Handling Pressure:**
   - ✓ Crisis Management: The ability to stay calm under pressure, a skill acquired in flag football, can be invaluable in crisis management situations in personal and professional life.
   - ✓ Entrepreneurship: Entrepreneurs often face high-pressure situations. Learning to thrive in such conditions can benefit those pursuing business ventures.

5. **Time Management:**
   - ✓ Balancing Act: Juggling flag football commitments with other responsibilities is akin to managing work, family, and personal life. Effective time management leads to a balanced lifestyle.
   - ✓ Project Management: Time management skills are essential in project management roles, where meeting deadlines is crucial to success.

6. **Communication Skills:**
   - ✓ Leadership Communication: Effective communication skills are vital for leaders and managers, enabling them to convey ideas, motivate teams, and foster positive working relationships.
   - ✓ Conflict Resolution: Strong communication skills can facilitate conflict resolution in personal relationships and the workplace.

7. **Goal Setting and Achievement:**
   - ✓ Personal Development: Applying goal-setting techniques from flag football to personal growth can help individuals pursue and achieve their ambitions.
   - ✓ Career Advancement: Goal-oriented individuals often set and achieve career objectives, leading to professional success.

8. **Sportsmanship and Fair Play:**
   - ✓ Community Engagement: Embracing sportsmanship principles can extend to community involvement and volunteering, promoting fairness and equity in various initiatives.

✓ Conflict Resolution: The ability to handle victories and losses gracefully can contribute to maintaining positive relationships in all aspects of life.

These are just a few examples of how the life skills cultivated through flag football can have far-reaching effects on personal growth and development. The principles of teamwork, leadership, resilience, and effective communication, among others, serve as valuable assets in navigating the complexities of life, relationships, and career pursuits. The holistic lessons learned on the flag football field empower individuals to excel not only as athletes but also as well-rounded, adaptable, and successful individuals in all areas of life.

❖ **Inspiring Stories from Fellow Players:** Sometimes, the most powerful motivation comes from hearing the experiences of those who have thrived in the sport. We'll share inspiring stories from fellow flag football players who have faced adversity, overcome challenges, and achieved remarkable success. These narratives inspire aspiring young players, demonstrating that dedication and perseverance can lead to outstanding accomplishments both on and off the field. These personal stories underscore the transformative potential of flag football in shaping lives.

Inspiring stories from fellow flag football players:
1. **From Doubt to Victory:**
   ✓ Sarah's journey in flag football is a story of determination and perseverance. When she first joined her flag football team, she faced skepticism and doubt from her

peers, who questioned her ability to compete in a predominantly male sport. However, Sarah didn't let this deter her. She dedicated herself to improving her skills, attending extra practices, and seeking guidance from experienced players and coaches. Over time, her hard work paid off as she became a skilled player and a respected leader on her team. Her story teaches us that one can overcome doubts and succeed in any endeavor with unwavering determination and a strong work ethic.

2. **The Power of Inclusivity:**

- ✓ David's story highlights the inclusivity and supportive nature of flag football. Despite having a physical disability, David's passion for the sport led him to an inclusive flag football league. At first, he faced unique challenges adapting his playing style and navigating the field. However, with the encouragement of his teammates and coaches, he persevered. His determination and positive attitude inspired those around him, and he became integral to his team's success. David's story serves as a reminder that flag football is a sport where everyone, regardless of their physical abilities, can find a place to belong and excel.

3. **Leadership On and Off the Field:**

- ✓ Jessica's transformation from a shy and reserved player to a confident leader is a testament to the personal growth that flag football can foster. Over time, Jessica developed her skills on the field and embraced leadership roles within her team. She learned to motivate and unite her teammates, creating a sense of camaraderie and teamwork that propelled her team to victory. Jessica's story demonstrates that flag football builds physical skills and cultivates leadership qualities that can positively impact both on and off the field.

4. **Overcoming Adversity:**

    ✓ Mark's journey is a story of resilience and determination. Mark refused to give up after a severe injury left him sidelined and uncertain about his future in flag football. He embarked on a rigorous rehabilitation journey, working tirelessly to regain strength and mobility. His determination and unwavering commitment to recovery paid off when Mark returned triumphantly to the sport. Not only did he return to the field, but he also played a pivotal role in leading his team to a championship victory. Mark's story serves as a potent reminder that setbacks can be overcome with perseverance and a positive mindset.

5. **Pursuing a Passion:**

    ✓ Emily's story is a testament to the transformative power of passion and initiative. Growing up in a community where flag football was not widely played, Emily took it upon herself to start her own team. Despite initial challenges in recruiting players and organizing practices, Emily's passion and determination prevailed. Her efforts led to establishing of a thriving flag football league in her area, allowing countless young girls to participate in the sport they love. Emily's story illustrates that vision, determination, and a commitment to one's passion can create positive change and open doors for others.

These inspiring stories highlight the incredible journeys of these flag football players and emphasize the broader life lessons that the sport imparts. They inspire young players to embrace challenges, believe in themselves, lead with integrity, overcome adversity, and pursue their passions. These narratives remind us that flag football is more than just a game; it's a vehicle for personal growth, empowerment, and lasting impact.

As you progress to becoming a skilled and confident flag football player, this comprehensive guide will remain your steadfast companion. It will continue to provide you with valuable insights, strategies, and inspiration every step of the way. Together, we will explore the expansive world of flag football, connect with its vibrant and supportive community, and empower young girls to shine on the field. Flag football is more than a sport; it's a pathway to personal growth and a culture that values inclusivity, teamwork, and lifelong learning.

Here's an expanded list of key flag football terminology with explanations:

❖ Flag Football: A non-contact version of American football where players wear flags that defenders must remove to down the ball carrier instead of tackling.

❖ Field: The rectangular playing area where flag football games occur, typically 70 yards in length and 25-30 yards in width.

❖ End Zone: The area at each end of the field, usually 10 yards deep, where teams aim to score touchdowns.

❖ Touchdown: The primary way to score is achieved when a player carries the ball into the opponent's end zone or when a receiver catches a pass in the end zone.

❖ Extra Point: An additional scoring opportunity after a touchdown, typically worth one point for a pass or two points for a run or pass into the end zone from a short distance.

❖ Conversion Attempt: The play used to try to earn extra points after a touchdown.

❖ Center: The player snaps the ball to the quarterback to initiate each play.

❖ Quarterback (QB): The offensive player responsible for receiving the snap, passing, and directing the team's offense.

❖ Running Back (RB): A player who carries the ball and can be a receiver. There may be multiple running backs on the field.

❖ Wide Receiver (WR): Offensive players who run pass routes and attempt to catch passes from the quarterback.

❖ Offensive Line: The players protect the quarterback and create running lanes for ball carriers.

❖ Defensive Line: The players aiming to pressure the quarterback and stop running plays.

- ❖ Line of Scrimmage: An imaginary line on the field where the ball is placed before each play. Both teams must remain behind this line until the play starts.
- ❖ Flag Belt: A belt worn by players with one or more flags attached. Defenders must remove a ball carrier's flag to down them.
- ❖ Flag Guarding: An illegal move where the ball carrier uses their hands or arms to shield or prevent defenders from pulling their flags.
- ❖ Fumble: When a player loses possession of the ball, which becomes free for either team to recover.
- ❖ Interception: When a defensive player catches a pass intended for an offensive player.
- ❖ Pass Rush: Defensive players attempt to pressure the quarterback and disrupt passing plays.
- ❖ Blitz: A defensive strategy where additional players rush the quarterback to increase pressure.
- ❖ Zone Coverage: A defensive strategy where defenders cover specific field areas rather than individual players.
- ❖ Man-to-Man Coverage: A defensive strategy where each defender is responsible for covering a specific offensive player.
- ❖ Touch (Down): When a defender successfully removes a ball carrier's flag, it counts as a "touch," indicating that the ball carrier is down.
- ❖ Offside: When a player crosses the line of scrimmage before the snap, resulting in a penalty.

- Penalty: An infraction of the rules that results in awarding yards or downs to the opposing team.

- Two-Point Conversion: A play attempt from a short distance that, if successful, earns two extra points following a touchdown.

- Turnover: When an offensive team loses possession of the ball to the opposing team, often due to an interception or fumble.

- Huddle: When the offensive team gathers to receive the play call from the quarterback.

- Pitch: A lateral pass from one player to another, often used in trick or option plays.

- Flag Pulling: Removing the opponent's flag to down the ball carrier.

- Snap: The act of the center delivering the ball to the quarterback to begin a play.

- Running Lane: A designated path for ball carriers to follow to advance the ball.

- Catching Zone: An area where receivers aim to catch passes from the quarterback.

- Pylon: A marker placed at the corners of the end zone, used to determine whether a player has scored a touchdown.

- Touchback: When the ball carrier downs the ball in their end zone, the opposing team gains possession at the 20-yard line.

- Passing Lane: A clear path for the quarterback to make a pass without interference from defenders.

- ❖ Rush Line: The line of scrimmage where defenders must start behind until the ball is snapped.
- ❖ Hike: The verbal signal used by the quarterback to request the snap from the center.
- ❖ Lateral: A backward pass moves the ball horizontally across the field.
- ❖ Draw Play: A deceptive running play that appears to be a pass initially.
- ❖ Play Clock: The time limit players have to snap the ball once the play is called.
- ❖ Shotgun Formation: A formation where the quarterback lines up several yards behind the center to receive the snap.
- ❖ End-Around: A trick play where the ball carrier takes a handoff and runs around the end of the offensive line.
- ❖ Safety: When the ball carrier is downed in their end zone, resulting in two points for the opposing team.
- ❖ Double Coverage: A defensive strategy where two defenders cover a single receiver to minimize their chances of catching a pass.
- ❖ Flag Grab: A defensive move where a player grabs an opponent's flag to down them.
- ❖ Ineligible Receiver: A player who cannot legally receive a pass due to their position on the field during the snap.
- ❖ Flag Penalty: A penalty resulting from an illegal action related to flag football rules.
- ❖ Passing Tree: A set of predetermined routes receivers run during a play.

❖ Sideline: The boundary marking the edge of the field, typically out of bounds.

❖ Hail Mary: A desperation pass play, often used when time is running out in a game, where the quarterback throws the ball deep into the end zone in hopes of a miraculous catch.

Understanding these terms will give you a comprehensive knowledge of flag football, enhancing your ability to communicate effectively and excel in the game.

Here are some trivia questions related to female flag football:

✓ Who is often regarded as one of the pioneers of women's flag football and has been instrumental in promoting the sport among females?

✓ In which year did the first official women's flag football league or tournament take place, and where was it held?

✓ Name a prominent female flag football player who has also represented her country in international competitions.

✓ What are the key differences between men's and women's flag football rules?

✓ Can you name a college or university known for its successful women's flag football program?

✓ What strategies do female flag football teams often employ to overcome potential physical disadvantages compared to male players?

- ✓ Which female flag football teams or organizations have made significant strides in promoting inclusivity and diversity within the sport?
- ✓ In women's flag football, what is the significance of having versatile players who can both run routes effectively and pull flags on defense?
- ✓ What are some of the challenges female flag football players may face in terms of funding, resources, and recognition, and how have they been addressed?
- ✓ Are there any international women's flag football tournaments or championships, and if so, which countries typically excel in the sport at the global level?

Here are the answers to the female flag football trivia questions:

- ✓ One of the pioneers of women's flag football and a promoter of the sport among females is Phyllis Merhige, who played a significant role in its development.
- ✓ The first official women's flag football league or tournament took place in 1971 in Miami, Florida.
- ✓ One prominent female flag football player who has represented her country in international competitions is Heather Furr.
- ✓ Some key differences between men's and women's flag football rules include variations in contact rules, field size, and sometimes the number of players on the field.
- ✓ The University of West Florida is known for its successful women's flag football program.

- ✓ Female flag football teams often emphasize speed, agility, and teamwork to overcome potential physical disadvantages compared to male players.
- ✓ The Women's Football Alliance (WFA) and the Independent Women's Football League (IWFL) are organizations that have made significant strides in promoting inclusivity and diversity within the sport.
- ✓ In women's flag football, versatile players who can both run routes effectively and pull flags on defense are essential for a well-rounded team.
- ✓ Female flag football players may face challenges related to funding, resources, and recognition, which are being addressed through increased visibility, advocacy, and support from organizations.
- ✓ Yes, there are international women's flag football tournaments and championships. Countries like the United States, Canada, and Mexico have excelled in the sport at the global level, with competitions such as the International Federation of American Football (IFAF) Women's World Championship showcasing their talent.

EMPOWERING

YOUNG GIRLS IN

FLAG

FOOTBALL

COMPREHENSIVE

GUIDE

BY Tommie Womack

Made in the USA
Las Vegas, NV
19 December 2024

14752982R00083